CHILDHOOD LOSS AND GRIEF

Guidelines for Educators and Professionals

Dr. Elena Merenda

CHILDHOOD LOSS AND GRIEF

Guidelines for Educators and Professionals

Dr. Elena Merenda

First published in 2020
as part of the Learner Book Imprint
http://doi.org/10.18848/978-1-86335-207-9/CGP (Full Book)

BISAC Codes: EDU023000, EDU048000, FAM014000

Common Ground Research Networks
2001 South First Street, Suite 202
University of Illinois Research Park
Champaign, IL
61820

Copyright © Elena Merenda 2020

All rights reserved. Apart from fair dealing for the purposes of study, research, criticism or review as permitted under the applicable copyright legislation, no part of this book may be reproduced by any process without written permission from the publisher.

Library of Congress Cataloging-in-Publication Data

Names: Merenda, Elena, author.
Title: Childhood loss and grief : guidelines for educators and
    professionals / Elena Merenda.
Description: Champaign : Common Ground Research Networks, 2020. | Includes
    bibliographical references. | Summary: "Loss is a universal experience
    of change- an experience that begins at birth and continues throughout
    life. Loss, of any kind, can have a profound effect on children. This
    book describes the commonalities and unique experience of childhood
    loss. Specifically, the five stages of grief are defined, and used as a
    framework for understanding grief and a process that children may
    experience with various types of losses. This book focuses on loss
    through death, divorce, and childhood illness, and the cultural and
    religious aspects of death and the grieving process. As educators are
    critical sources of support for grieving children, this book supports
    educators in recognizing children's significant symptoms of grief, it
    provides strategies for including death and loss in the curriculum, and
    it makes suggestions for talking to children about death. There is an
    additional section of therapeutic play experiences for educators to use
    in their own practice"-- Provided by publisher.
Identifiers: LCCN 2020007833 (print) | LCCN 2020007834 (ebook) | ISBN
    9781863352055 (hardback) | ISBN 9781863352062 (paperback) | ISBN
    9781863352079 (pdf)
Subjects: LCSH: Grief in children. | Loss (Psychology) in children
Classification: LCC BF723.G75 M47 2020 (print) | LCC BF723.G75 (ebook) |
    DDC 155.9/37083--dc23
LC record available at https://lccn.loc.gov/2020007833
LC ebook record available at https://lccn.loc.gov/2020007834

Cover Photo Credit: Elena Merenda

TABLE OF CONTENTS

Introduction 1

Chapter 1 5
Loss and Grief

Chapter 2 11
Grief, Mourning, and Bereavement

Chapter 3 21
Cultural and Religious Aspects of Grieving

Chapter 4 33
The Death of a Parent

Chapter 5 85
Divorce

Chapter 6 97
The Parentified Child

Chapter 7 103
How Life-Threatening Illnesses Affect Children

Chapter 8 125
Responding to Grieving Children in the Classroom

References 155

Introduction

Source: Pixabay

"I loved you like there was no tomorrow, and then one day there wasn't."
-Unknown

It is important for me to share research on childhood grief and the support grieving children require from educators because my father died when I was sixteen years old and support from my teachers at the time was nonexistent. My father was diagnosed with Lymphoma. His cancer began with a tumor on his spine and one year later, it ended with sorrow for my mom, my two younger sisters who were ten and thirteen at the time, and me. At an age when life already seemed so complicated, it suddenly became insufferable for me. I remained home from school for two weeks after my father died. I remember feeling scared to go back to school because I did not know how I would be treated or what other students would say about me. I was also unsure about how my teachers would treat me. The last thing I wanted was for them to expect less of me because of my circumstances. To my surprise and eventual disbelief and disappointment, my loss was not even acknowledged by any of my teachers. I remember walking into my first class and feeling embarrassed because the other students were looking at me and talking to each other about "the girl whose father died." At a time when I needed someone to talk to, the teachers' lack of acknowledgement left me feeling alienated and alone.

I was not the only child in my family to experience a difficult return to school. The middle child, who was thirteen at the time, also returned to school two weeks after my father died. The day of her return was the first time since my dad's funeral that she saw her best friend. Upon my sister's arrival, her best friend hugged her and welcomed her back to school. In a matter of minutes, my sister and her friend were taken to the principal's office and my mom was called to take my sister home because she broke the "hands off" rule. At a time when my sister needed a hug and to feel welcomed, she was made to feel belittled. You can only imagine how my mother felt when she was called to retrieve her daughter for hugging her friend after the death of her father.

Children, at any age, should not feel alone, alienated, or unsupported by their educators at such a difficult time in their lives. I truly believe my grief experience would have been very different had I received some emotional support from the adults with whom I spent most of my day. The purpose of this book is to provide educators with a snapshot of how children grieve various losses and to provide educators with knowledge and skills to enable them to support grieving students.

The death of a parent is likely the most difficult loss that a child can experience because parents are the most important people in a child's life (Silverman, 2000). For the vast majority of children, parents remain children's most significant others. Parents typically support their children, both physically and emotionally; parents provide a secure home environment in which children can grow and mature; and parents act both as the children's protectors and as their models (Worden, 1996). Immediately after birth, infants begin to develop an attachment to their parents or caregiver in order for social and emotional development to occur. Parental responses to this relationship lead to the development of attachment, which further supports the development of the child's emotions, thoughts, and feelings (Silverman, 2000). Essentially, parents are negotiating the necessary developmental tasks that will bring children to adulthood (Worden, 1996). When a parent dies, the child loses a key relationship; thus, creating profound change in the child's social, emotional, and cognitive capacity. The child loses a significant person in his or her life, as well as the sense of security that existed in that relationship (Silverman, 2000). The loss of a parent to death and the effects the parent's death has in the home and in the family, changes the very heart of the child's existence (Worden, 1996).

Whether or not children grieve has long been debated (Bowlby, 1963; Wolfenstein, 1966; Furman, 1974; Worden, 1996, McGuiness, 2011). However, the most common conclusion is that while children vary in their emotional and behavioural reactions, children of all ages grieve (McGuinness, 2011). Worden developed four tasks of mourning children proceed through after the loss of a parent (Worden, 1996). The first task is to accept the reality of the loss. Similar to adults, children must believe their parent is dead and will not return before they can deal with the emotional impact of a loss. This acknowledgement requires the child to comprehend the finality and irreversibility of death. The second task is to experience the pain or emotional aspects of the loss. It is necessary for children to acknowledge and work through their emotions associated with the loss of their parent; otherwise, these emotions will manifest in other ways, including irregular behaviour patterns. The third task is to adjust to an environment in which the parent is missing. The achievement of this adjustment is determined by the roles and relationships that the deceased parent played in the child and family's life. An aspect of the mourning process includes adapting to the loss of these roles, with the death of the parent. The fourth task is to relocate the dead person within one's life and find ways to memorialize the person. There is a widely accepted belief that bereaved individuals must let go of the deceased, and while this may be moderately true, it is also true that one never forgets a meaningful relationship. As a result, the task does not require bereaved children to give up the relationship with the deceased parent. Rather, the task is to find a new and appropriate place for the parent in the children's lives. While there is a wide range of normal responses to the death of a parent, each child will negotiate these tasks in his or her own individual way, and the personal circumstances of each child will influence the way in which he or she ultimately deals with the loss (Worden, 1996). Furthermore, there are many determinants to children's adjustment to the loss of a parent; therefore, each child's adjustment will look different.

According to Cohen and Mannarino (2011), educators are critical sources of support for children who are grieving the loss of a parent. However, educators often feel uncomfortable discussing death and loss with children (Naierman, 1997). Since educators spend so much time interacting with children, they play a vital role in helping children understand and transcend their grief (Naierman, 1997). Educators may be the first and only adults to recognize children's significant symptoms of grief because grieving parents are often too overwhelmed with their own loss to recognize their children's loss (Cohen & Mannarino, 2011). An awareness that children grieve and knowledge of the grieving process and its manifestation in children is crucial in the field of early childhood studies because it prepares practitioners and professionals with the skills needed to provide effective support and interventions to grieving children and their families (Naierman, 1997). "Educators who understand the grief process and its manifestations in children can provide the continuity, security, and support that grieving students so desperately need" (Naierman, 1997, p. 62).

CHAPTER 1

Loss and Grief

Source: Pixabay

"Grief is in two parts. The first is loss. The second is the remaking of life."
-Anne Roiphe

DEFINING LOSS

Loss is a universal experience of change and it begins at the moment of birth. The fetus is housed in a warm, dark, fully functioning uterus for approximately nine months. It is able to listen to sounds from outside the mother's body. It is soothed by the sound of the mother's heartbeat. It is safe. This safety all comes to an end at the moment of birth. The newborn arrives and is taken, cleaned, wrapped, and placed in the mother's arms. Although the newborn is returned to his or her mother, a loss has taken place and something new is offered (Mongelluzzo, 2013; Kubler-Ross & Kessler, 2005).

When you think about loss, especially in terms of loss in the lives of children, people often think of death. It is important that we understand that there is no shortage of opportunities to experience loss in a lifetime. Everything that involves change involves loss. You have experienced many losses in your life. You were born, then you gave up being carried when you learned to walk, you gave up being fed when you learned to eat independently, you gave up diapers when you learned to use the toilet, you learned to leave your home and parents with courage and strength when you started kindergarten. As you can see, loss is an everyday experience and it is a part of the typical development of children. Therefore, it can and will enter the lives of the children early childhood professionals work with.

Research has shown profound effects of loss during childhood, as indicated in the table below (Mongelluzzo, 2013; Kubler-Ross & Kessler, 2005).

TYPES OF LOSSES FOR CHILDREN

From the time of birth, children form assumptions about the way the world works. Often, these assumptions are positive and adaptive, and these assumptions help them predict the world around them (Mongelluzzo, 2013; Kubler-Ross & Kessler, 2005).

When children experience loss, their assumptions about the way the world works may be more negative, or positive assumptions they once held may be threatened by the loss (Mongelluzzo, 2013; Kubler-Ross & Kessler, 2005). "The abused or neglected child may assume that adults hurt you or won't be there when you need something. The child who faces the death of a parent or sibling has the assumption of the security of the family shattered. The child with specific learning difficulties may assume that it's not worth trying because you still won't succeed. The child who has trouble making friends or is bullied may assume that it is safer to be your own company, to reject others, or to start exerting control by bullying others. The child who lives with chronic illness or becomes seriously ill may not assume that it is worth planning for, or working toward a future. The child hurt in an accident may stop assuming that it is safe to be outside your home" (Mongelluzzo, 2013, p. 25)

Chapter One: Loss and Grief

Type of Loss	Effects found in Research Studies
Childhood abuse and neglect	Psychopathology, criminal behaviour, sexual dysfunction and promiscuity, relationship problems, substance abuse
Parental death	Anxiety, social withdrawal and problems, lower self-esteem and self-efficacy
Sibling death	Behaviour problems, reduced social competence, anger, sense of responsibility
Peer death	Anger, distress, confusion, difficulty talking about death, disenfranchised grief
Chronic illness	Social problems, anxiety
Parental separation/divorce	Social problems, alcohol and nicotine usage etc.
Refugee status	Social problems, anxiety
Homelessness	Suicidal ideation
Victims of crime	Anxiety, PTSD

Adapted from Murray, 2005

As you can see in the figure below, when children feel unsafe due to a loss, they may become angry, confused, and fearful, requiring them to seek security from others. Children may correct this feeling of insecurity by rearranging and reorganizing the world to what they are able to control. This often leads to behaviours such as eating disorders, tantrums, and in severe cases, cutting (Mongelluzzo, 2013; Kubler-Ross & Kessler, 2005).

Source: Merenda

Childhood Loss and Grief

While there are many commonalities in the process of loss for children, every child is unique and experiences loss differently. Below are some factors that may affect loss in the lives of children (Mongelluzzo, 2013; Kubler-Ross & Kessler, 2005).

EFFECTS OF FEELING UNSAFE ON CHILDREN

Gender

Western culture socializes boys and girls to react to loss differently. Boys typically are withdrawn; stifle emotions; express their feelings with anger and aggression; maintain silence instead of vocalizing their emotions; repress guilt; distance themselves from the thoughts of what happened (McKissock, 1998; Staudacher, 1991).

Girls typically act out their grief through nurturing caring behaviour; cry more; have difficulty concentrating; become more anxious; confide in their friends; talk about their loss; acknowledge their loss and grief (McKissock, 1998; Staudacher, 1991).

Relationship with the Lost Object

Attachment theories suggest that the relationship with the lost object prior to the loss will affect the relationship with the lost object after the loss. Part of the process of grieving and mourning the loss is being able to form attachments with new objects.

Source: Min An

Circumstances in which the Loss Occurred

Anticipated loss refers to an expected loss. For example, the loss of someone who has been ill for much time and has been told by doctors that they have only a short

Chapter One:Loss and Grief

lifespan left. ***Unanticipated loss*** refers to a sudden, unexpected loss. For example, a car accident, a heart attack, or a stroke.

DEFINING GRIEF

Loss refers to something that has changed and ***grief*** is the process of dealing with that change. Everyone grieves differently depending on the type of thing, person, or place that is lost. Kubler-Ross (2005) developed five stages of grief, as depicted below, that outlines the typical responses to loss. The five stages- denial, anger, bargaining, depression, and acceptance- are the five stages that make up the process. The stages were developed as tools to help grieving individuals frame and identify their feelings, with an understanding that everyone grieves differently and grief is not a linear timeline.

For the purpose of this book, ***grief*** will be defined as feelings and reactions that are a part of the natural process of coping with loss.

Five Stages

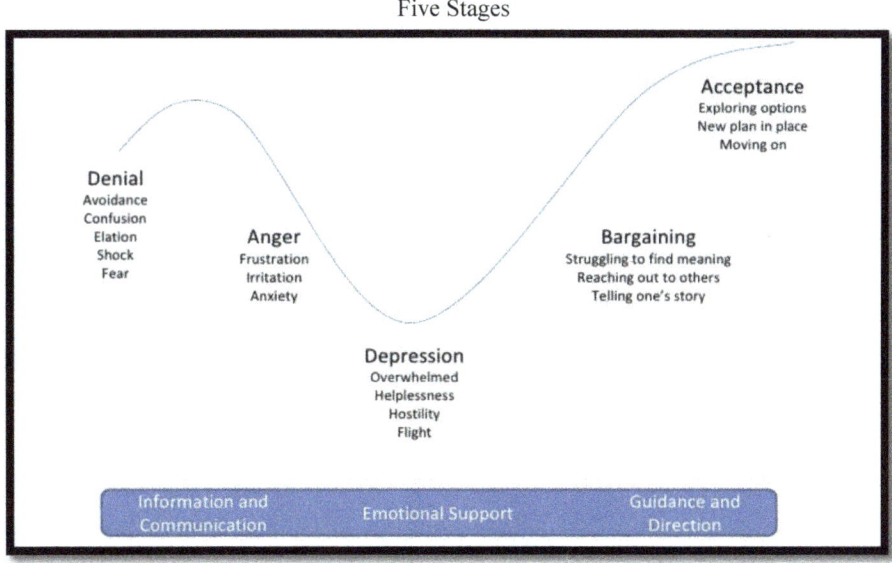

Source: Wikimedia Commons

Denial

Denial helps individuals to survive the loss. When in denial, the world becomes meaningless and overwhelming. Individuals go numb, and wonder how they can go on. Denial and shock help individuals to cope; survive the loss; and progress through their feelings of grief (Mongelluzzo, 2013; Kubler-Ross & Kessler, 2005).

Anger

Anger is a necessary and common stage of grief. Individuals may be angry at the person who left, or angry at themselves for allowing the loss to happen (Mongelluzzo, 2013; Kubler-Ross & Kessler, 2005).

Bargaining

Eventually, individuals who are grieving find themselves bargaining, trying to get back what they lost. The bargain might be directed to a higher power/religious figure, to the person/object that was lost, or anyone who might seem to have power over the situation. For example, a child might promise to clean their toys or stop arguing with their siblings in order to get back what was lost (Mongelluzzo, 2013; Kubler-Ross & Kessler, 2005).

Depression

Depression after a loss is often considered unnatural; something that needs to be fixed, something to snap out of. However, depression is an appropriate response to loss. Depression can present as any of the following symptoms: sadness, frequent crying, changes in your appetite or sleep patterns, and unexplained aches and pains (Mongelluzzo, 2013; Kubler-Ross & Kessler, 2005).

Acceptance

Acceptance is the last stage of grief, when the individual has accepted the reality of the loss and recognizes that the new reality is the permanent reality. During this stage, individuals understand what they have lost and recognize how important that thing or person was to them; however, they no longer feel angry about it, and they're finished with bargaining to get it back (Mongelluzzo, 2013; Kubler-Ross & Kessler, 2005).

CHAPTER 2

Grief, Mourning, and Bereavement

Source: Pexels

"Mourning is love with no place to go."
-Anonymous

McGoldrick (2004) stated, "Death is a central experience of life, one that the dominant American culture has not dealt with very well" (p. 82). Unfortunately, this cultural avoidance of death has caused educators to feel reluctant to discuss death in the classroom because childhood grief is misunderstood. There are cultural variations in how death is expected to be experienced and discussed, and as such, death is viewed as a forbidden topic of conversation to be had with children. However, 1 in 20 children experience the loss of a parent before the age of 18 (Andrea Warnick Consulting, 2016); therefore, it is important for educators to build confidence and empathy in talking about death with children and supporting them through their grief. In order for educators to understand childhood grief and feel comfortable talking to children about death, educators should first develop a general understanding of grief, mourning, and bereavement.

CHILDREN GRIEVING THE DEATH OF A LOVED ONE

Loss can be defined as the end of a relationship between an individual and someone or something to whom or to which that individual has become attached. Loss can include a physical loss (death), a social loss (terminated employment) or a symbolic loss (divorce). Terms used to refer to individuals coping with loss include bereavement, grief, and mourning. Although these terms are often used interchangeably and are obviously related, there are differences in their meaning (Doka, 2010).

According to Steen (1998), **bereavement** is the *internal process* that takes place after having lost a significant person in one's life. It is a *human experience* that can be potentially harmful to an individual's health because a bereaved individual may experience psychological, social, and physical stress as a result of losing an important person in his or her life (Kirwin & Hamrin, 2005). Although every individual bereaves differently, Cutcliffe (1998) and Webb (2010) describe three universal elements essential for defining bereavement experiences. First, a relationship with a person that is valued; second, the loss, ending, termination, separation of that relationship; and third, a survivor deprived by the loss.

While bereavement is the human experience connected to losing a significant person in one's life, **mourning** is defined as the "...*mental work* following the loss of a loved object through death" (Furman, 1974, p. 34). Krueger (1983), states that in order for this mental work to be successful and for mourning to occur, the bereaved person must comprehend the "significance, seriousness, permanence, and irreversibility" of his or her loss (p. 590). Bowlby (1960) describes four phases of mourning, as indicated in the figure below. They are (1) numbing; (2) yearning and searching; (3) disorganization and despair; and (4) reorganization.

Chapter Two: Grief, Mourning, and Bereavement

Bowlby's Four Phases of Mourning

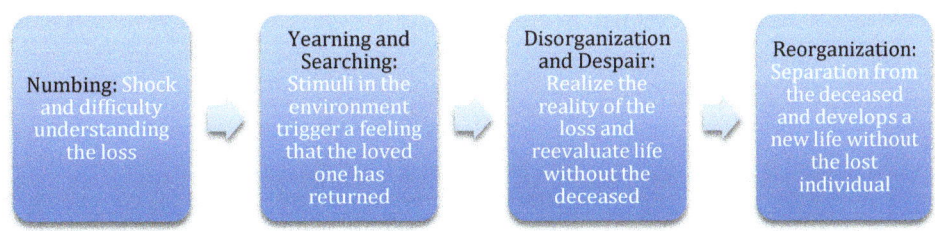

Source: Merenda

In addition to feeling typical grief reactions such as sadness and anger, a mourning individual must also understand that the deceased person will never return, but that life can continue to be meaningful without that person's physical presence. This acceptance of the irreversibility of loss is referred to by Bowlby (1960) as ***relinquishing the object.*** The mourning process, specifically the action of relinquishing the object, can be very difficult mental work. As a result of this difficulty, Rando (1993) developed a model called, ***Six "R" Processes of Mourning*** that facilitates healthy grieving.

Six "R" Processes of Mourning

The Six "R" Processes of Mourning	Description
1. Recognize the loss	The mourner needs to: • acknowledge that the death has occurred, and • understand the reasons for the occurrence of the death
2. React to the separation	The reality of the death is recognized, the mourner reacts to and copes with that reality: • Experiences the pain • Feels, identifies, accepts, and gives some form of expression to all the psychological reactions to the loss • Identifies and mourns secondary losses Unacknowledged and unexpressed emotions are major precipitants of complicated mourning.

The Six "R" Processes of Mourning	Description
3. Recollect and re-experience the deceased and the relationship	The mourner needs to change its attachment and their old assumptive world with the deceased in order to readjust. This is done through withdrawing their emotional investment from both by: a) Reviewing and remembering the deceased and the relationship realistically (including all attachment ties, such as needs, emotions, thoughts, behaviours, dreams, and expectations); and b) Reviving and re-experiencing the feelings associated with that which is remembered When remembering and feeling the connective emotions, the intensity of them lessens which loosens the ties with the deceased, ultimately leading to the next "R" processes, relinquishing the old ties.
4. Relinquish the old attachments to the deceased and the old assumptive world	Loosening the ties with the deceased doesn't mean that the deceased is forgotten or unloved. Rather it means that the ties are modified to reflect the change that the loved one is now dead and cannot return the mourner's emotional investment or gratify his or her needs as before.
5. Readjust to move adaptively into the new world without forgetting the old	Once the ties are loosened, the mourner is at liberty to take steps towards readjustment. This includes internal and external changes to permit the event and its consequences to fit into his or her life: a) revising the assumptive world b) developing a new relationship with the deceased c) adopting new ways of being in the world, and d) forming a new identity
6. Reinvest	The mourner reinvests in the new life without the deceased one. The emotional energy that formerly had been directed toward the preservation and maintenance of the relationship with the deceased one now must be redirected toward rewarding new investments in other people, objects, roles, hopes, beliefs, goals etc. The reinvestment need not be in a duplicate of what was lost (e.g. a widower does not have to marry a new wife). Rather, the sole requirement is that the emotional energy be reinvested where it can be returned to the mourner.

Adapted from Solomon & Rando, 2014

Key Terms

Loss: the end of a relationship between an individual and someone or something to whom or to which that individual has become attached

Bereavement: the internal process that takes place after having lost a significant person in one's life. It is a human experience that can be potentially harmful to an individual's health because a bereaved individual may experience psychological, social, and physical stress as a result of losing an important person in his or her life

Mourning: the mental work following the loss of a loved object through death. It is taking the internal experience of grief and expressing it

Grief: the emotional response to loss including reactions in feelings, in physical sensations, in cognitions, and in behaviours

Source: Merenda

GRIEF THEORY

Although the terms *bereavement* and *mourning* are closely related to the term *grief*, grief theory has a much longer and detailed history. In Western cultures, the beginning of a modern theory of the process of grief is credited to Freud. In 1917, during the development of psychoanalysis, Freud proposed that people needed to work through the loss of a loved one by emotionally detaching from the deceased and letting go of hopes for a future relationship with the deceased individual. Freud anticipated that grieving involves a process of *hypercathecting* and then *decathecting* the internal image of the deceased person. In other words, the grieving individual would stay closely attached to the deceased person and eventually begin to detach from the relationship he or she had with the deceased person. Subsequent psychoanalytic theorists such as Bowlby carried Freud's theory forward which led to the development of a definition and understanding of grief (Rothaupt & Becker, 2007).

In more modern approaches, **grief** is defined as the <u>emotional response</u> to loss including reactions in feelings, in physical sensations, in cognitions, and in behaviours (Kirwin & Hamrin, 2005; Webb, 2010). Grief is considered a process rather than a specific emotion like fear or sadness and it can be expressed by a variety of thoughts, emotions, and behaviours (Wolfelt, 1983). Bowlby (1960) describes grief as "...the sequence of subjective states that follow loss and accompany mourning" (p. 11).

WORKING THROUGH THE GRIEVING PROCESS

Webb (2010) outlines three tasks for working through the grief process. First, one must release oneself from his or her connection with the deceased. When a person loves someone, he or she is emotionally bonded to that person. This is called *cathexis*. When this loved one dies, the individual left behind has to release his or her connection to the deceased as a result of the death. Consequently, the living individual develops an altered attachment with the deceased in the form of memories. Second, one must readjust to the environment because the deceased is missing. The person who is grieving must develop a new view of the world and lifestyle without the loved one. The person may need to redefine his or her roles and skills to incorporate the roles and skills the deceased individual used to perform. For example, a bereaved husband may need to take on the unfamiliar role of cooking dinner or bringing the children to school, if the wife was responsible for these tasks. Third, the remaining individual must form a new relationship; the emotional energy that is displaced from the relationship with the deceased is reinvested in someone or something else.

FACTORS THAT INFLUENCE THE GRIEVING PROCESS

According to Webb (2010), how individuals respond to loss and how they complete the tasks of grieving depends in part on whether the loss was anticipated or not. ***Anticipatory grief*** refers to grief reactions experienced prior to an expected loss; for example, how one might respond to the approaching death of a terminally ill loved one (Webb, 2010). According to Fulton and Fulton (1971), aspects of anticipatory grief include depression, a heightened concern for the ill loved one, and preparation for the death. Fulton and Fulton (1971) further suggest that although these aspects of anticipatory grief can be difficult, anticipatory grief has its benefits over unanticipated grief because it allows for completing unfinished business by expressing feelings and resolving past issues, as well as providing time to prepare for and absorb the reality of the loss. On the other hand, ***unanticipated grief*** often evokes complex grief reactions resulting from a sudden, unexpected loss. The griever may then experience complicated grief reactions (Fulton & Fulton, 1971). Worden (1991) listed several factors that interfere with the grief process; the type of relationship the individual had with the deceased, the circumstances that surrounded the death, the bereaved person's past experiences with complicated grief, the bereaved person's character and how he or she copes with emotional distress, the support system surrounding the bereaved individual, and if the bereaved person and those around him or her act as if the loss did not happen. Grief work involves not only grieving the loss of the loved one, but it also includes grieving the loss of all that made their relationship, with the hopes, dreams, and goals that the person had for the deceased (Doka, 2010).

Difficult grief work as described by Fulton and Fulton (1971) and Worden (1991) often leads to unresolved grief. ***Unresolved grief*** is a clinical condition characterized by "inhibition, suppression, or absence of grieving, exaggeration or distortion of elements of the normal grief process, and/or the prolongation of normal grieving" (Geller, 1985, p. 142). According to Rando (1984), there are seven forms of unresolved grief. These forms can overlap, and each has components of denial or regression. These seven forms of unresolved grief, as described in the subsequent figure, are absence of feelings of grief and mourning, embarrassment with/surrounding some of the normal symptoms of grief, such as fear and anger, delayed grief due to other responsibilities or obligations, conflicted grief involving manifestations of anger and extreme guilt, and chronic grief which includes intense grief reactions for a long period of time.

Seven Forms of Unresolved Grief

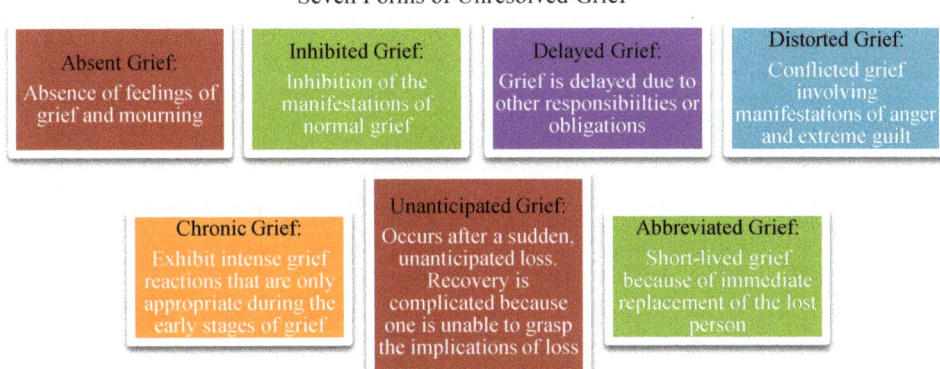

Source: Merenda

Similar to unresolved grief is complicated grief. **Complicated grief** is a "deviation from the normal grief experience in terms of…time…intensity or both" (Fujisawa et al., 2010, p. 352). Complicated grief includes expression of grief-related symptoms (searching for the deceased, loneliness, feelings of mistrust, anger, shock) beyond a time which is considered adaptive. As a result, an individual is unable to return to "his or her pre-loss level of functioning following bereavement experience" (Webb, 2010, p. 26).

Western Bereavement Theories

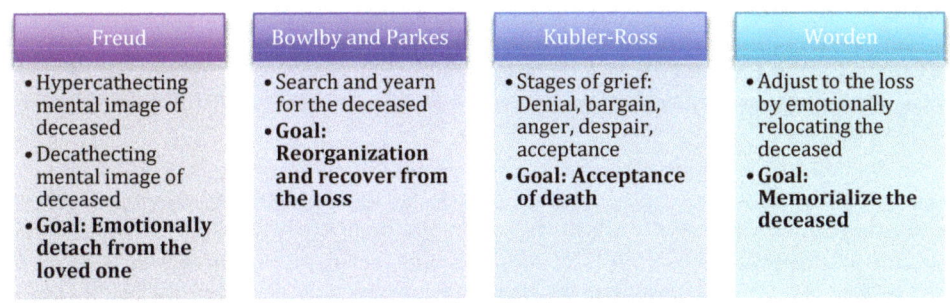

Adapted from Rothaupt & Becker

CHILDREN AND GRIEF

One in seven children from Western countries will experience a loss before the age of 20 and 1 in 20 Canadian children before the age of 18 will experience the death of a parent (Pidcock, Ashpole, & Warnick, 2015). Therefore, it is important for educators to understand the process of grief, mourning, and bereavement in order to adequately support bereaved children and families. It was once thought that children do not grieve; however, over time, research has proven that children have the ability to grieve despite their age. Bowlby proposed that children as young as 6 months of age are able to experience grief reactions resembling those seen in adults (Worden, 1996).

Furthermore, Wolfelt (1983) stated, "...grief does not focus on one's ability to 'understand', but instead upon one's ability to 'feel'. Therefore, any child mature enough to love is mature enough to grieve" (p. 20). The grief of young children is often ignored because of the misguided belief that children are too young to understand (Webb, 2010). Lack of knowledge and limited interest in the childhood grieving process has led to myths about childhood grief. The most common myth is that children do not grieve and that they recover quickly from a loss (Auman, 2007). Another myth is that children who experience parental death will grow up to be maladjusted adults (Auman, 2007). The most compelling myth is that it is best to protect children from death and grief (Auman, 2007). It is natural for adults to want to protect children from painful experiences, but children will grieve in their own unique ways and it is imperative that caring adults do not dictate or interrupt that process. Instead, adults should encourage and facilitate children's expression of grief (Fiorelli, 2002). As a result of these myths, children are regarded as *the forgotten mourners* (Auman, 2007).

In order to recognize children as mourners it is important to understand children's grief experiences. Children's grief is *cyclical*. With each new stage of development, the child may recycle and in some ways, revisit previous feelings and behaviours associated with the death itself (Willis, 2002). It is common for grief to periodically reappear over a lifetime, sometimes as a result of cognitive and emotional development, at other times it is triggered by emotional or physical indication, or in response to other losses. As children mature, the focus of their grief may shift from missing the deceased person to mourning what the person could have been to the child, and coming to terms with the person's own responsibility for his or her absence. Furthermore, the way in which children define the memory of the deceased may determine their level of adaptation and coping throughout childhood and adulthood (Hung & Rabin, 2009).

Second, while adults are better able to express themselves and ask for what they need, depending on their age, children often do not fully understand why they feel the way they do (Willis, 2002). Children's grief reactions are sporadic because children cannot thoroughly explore all their thoughts and feelings as rationally as adults can (Howarth, 2011). As a result of this inability to explore their thoughts and feelings, children often demonstrate what come to be seen as unacceptable behaviours, which are actually expressions of the child's confusion about what has happened. A variety of emotional reactions may be expected from a grieving child, including numbness, disbelief, yearning, anguish, anger, and guilt. Childhood grief reactions may also manifest in psychosomatic symptoms, temper tantrums, and academic failure (Howarth, 2011). According to Willis (2002), children often have difficulty verbally articulating their feelings about grief; thus, it is through their behaviour that they may demonstrate anger and fear of abandonment or death.

Third, adults have the life experience to understand that adjusting to the loss of a loved one gets easier over time, but the concept of time is less clear to young children. Children do not always understand that things usually get easier as time passes (Willis, 2002). As a result, children may feel abandonment and a loss of security and control in their lives (Naierman, 1997). Fourth, adults usually have some form of built-in support system that includes family and friends who help the bereaved adult cope (Willis, 2002). Unlike adults who may obtain comfort and support from the condolences of their family and friends, bereaved children may dread this process and often, their peers feel equally uncomfortable at the idea of having to speak to the bereaved child. The bereaved child's peers likely do not know what to say and maybe afraid that they or their friend will start crying (Webb, 2010). Furman (1974) comments that children consider crying a sign of immaturity and they believe crying makes them look infantile; therefore, bereaved children and their peers will often avoid discussions that may elicit crying.

NORMAL GRIEVING PROCESS

Although children grieve quite differently than adults, traditional grief theory states that children will adjust to their loss and be able to move on by completing certain tasks (McClatchy & Vonk, 2009; Worden & Silverman, 1993). Worden and Silverman (1996) emphasize that a normal grieving process for children includes specific tasks associated with common responses to loss over time. In their model, children must complete four tasks in order to adapt to the loss and reintegrate into a new life.

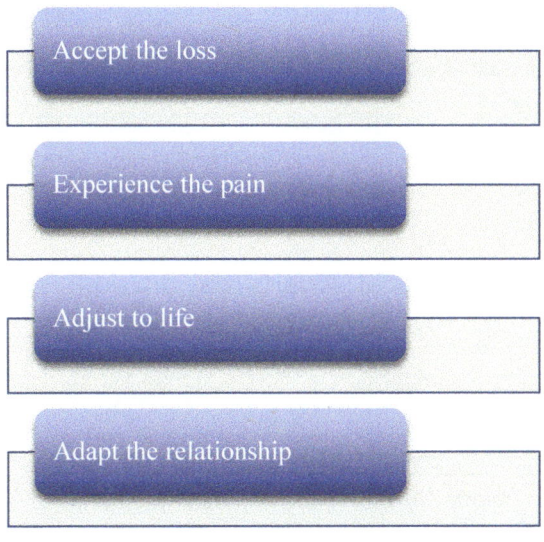

Source: Merenda

As shown in the preceding figure, the first task is to accept the reality and permanency of the loss (Worden & Silverman, 1993). Children of young ages are not cognitively able to understand death as adults do. They grieve without understanding what is happening to them because they have not had the experience of finality that accompanies someone's death (Fitzgerald, 2003). As a result, in order for children to accomplish this first task, children need accurate information about the death so they can avoid *magical thinking* or filling in the gaps with misinformation. Acceptance of the loss is very difficult because the process involves complete recognition that the deceased individual will not return.

The second task is children need to experience the pain and the emotional aspects of the loss. Intense emotions such as sadness, despair, anger, guilt, fear, loneliness, shame, and jealousy may all be part of this experience. These painful feelings may initially be constant, but they later become sporadic or intermittent, resurfacing at unexpected times, and causing the child to feel out of control. Eventually, the painful feelings become less frequent and they may only arise during anniversaries of the loss, holidays, and special events such as the deceased individual's birthday.

The third task is adjusting to life without the loved one. The difficulty of this task depends on the relationship between the child and the deceased individual and the amount of disruption the loss has caused in the child's daily life. Finally, the child must adapt the relationship with the deceased from one based on continuing interactions with the deceased to one based on memories.

Children gradually withdraw emotional energy from the lost loved one and focus on establishing new relationships with others (Worden & Silverman, 1996). Freud defined this withdrawal of emotional energy as ***decathexis*** (Christ, 2000). Worden and Silverman (1996) declare that releasing a central attachment to the deceased person allows for more room and energy to engage in the present life. Ultimately, the process outlined in Worden and Silverman's (1996) model is characterized by reconciliation. ***Reconciliation*** is defined as the process that occurs as the bereaved child works to move forward in life without the physical presence of the person who died. With reconciliation comes a capacity to be involved in the activities of living (Cohen et al., 2002).

According to Howarth (2011), all children, depending on their age, are generally able to cope with the normative grieving process without complications; however, some children who cannot successfully address the four tasks of grieving may suffer from complicated grief. ***Complicated grief*** has been identified as a combination of depression and grief-related symptoms that meddle with a child's ability to return to his or her life after a period of normal grieving (Mitchell et al., 2004; Prigerson et al., 1995). Goldman (2001) describes children with complicated grief as caught in *frozen blocks of time*, incapable of moving through the grief process because of overpowering feelings. Goldman (2001) also suggests that children can become "imprisoned in these feelings if they are not given the freedom to work through their grief" (p. 10). In order to assist and encourage children through the grieving process, professionals, caretakers, and parents need to provide a safe environment where the child can re-experience the loss of a loved one and all the associated feelings, without shame or fear of judgement.

CHAPTER 3

Cultural and Religious Aspects of Grieving

Source: Rebecca Swafford

"Death is just a change in address, but what you believe will determine what neighborhood you end up in."
-Anonymous

Any analysis of grief and the grieving process in childhood must include the cultural and religious beliefs in the child's home environment that have an impact on the grieving child (Webb, 2010). Children are highly influenced by the way that they are socialized. By observing others and responding to situations similarly, children of different cultures are found to limit their emotional response based on whether or not emotional expression is encouraged (Heath et. al, 2008). Grief felt for the loss of a loved one can occur across all ages and cultures; however, the role of culture in an individuals' experience of grief and mourning is not well understood by educators (Clements, Vigil, Manno, & Henry, 2003). McGoldrick et al. (1991) caution professionals to "...be careful about the definitions of 'normality' in assessing families' responses to death, [since] the manner of, as well as the length of time assumed normal for mourning differs greatly from culture to culture" (p. 176-177). The child absorbs and interprets the beliefs and customs maintained by their family and this influences the child's grieving process; therefore, it is especially important for educators to understand different cultural and religious beliefs about death, rituals, and acceptable mourning patterns (Webb, 2010).

Death is a universal experience and a certainty for members of all cultures; however, what people experience, believe, or feel after a loved one has died varies significantly across cultures and even within a culture (Clements, Vigil, Manno & Henry, 2003; Perkins, Cortez & Hazuda, 2009). Lopez (2011) defines culture as the way of life of a society, consisting of prescribed ways of behaving or norms of conduct, beliefs, values, and skills; it is the sum total of life patterns passed from generation to generation.

Culture is recognized as a key factor in understanding an individual's experience of loss, mourning, bereavement, and grief. Established cultural traditions of mourning may vary for practices such as decisions about burial or cremation, funeral or memorial services, acceptable lengths of time for grieving, expressions of grief and emotional responses of grievers, use of customs and rituals, and help seeking behaviours (Clements, Vigil, Manno & Henry, 2003; Lopez, 2011).

Grieving and death rituals are often heavily influenced by religion. Religions help people connect to one another and to the *Divine* as part of a healing process during the time of suffering. Religions also provide concepts, rituals, and values that help individuals find meaning and purpose, and cope with death and dying (Puchalski & O'Donnell, 2005). Religious faith addresses the existential questions of life and death (Lobar, Youngblut & Brooten, 2006; Walsh et al., 2002). Characteristics of religion that provide comfort to people after the death of a family member varies widely between cultures and within cultures, but all religions try to provide a purpose and meaning for human existence (Aiken, 2001).

Miraglia (2012) conducted interviews with two remaining parents.(Remaining? Please rephrase for clarity) The parents were asked about their religion and the influence religion has on their grief process. Mike is a secular Jew; however, he defined himself as more spiritual rather than religious. "I have thought about the soul...I have wondered about Silvana...if she is around, if she has a presence, if she saw the affect that her death had on the children". Mike explains that religion and these thoughts about the soul did not comfort him or his children because of the nature of his wife's death. "...if you're really religious and you really believe in religion, then no, that's not true [Silvana is not in heaven]. Silvana committed suicide; she's not in that place".

Judaism strictly forbids suicide and considers suicide to be a criminal act (Worchel & Gearing, 2010). "One who commits suicide is abhorred by Judaism as one who has denied the life given to them by God" (Robinson, 2000, p. 185). According to Kaplan and Shoenberg (1988) Judaic principles assign a spiritual consequence to suicide. When an individual commits suicide, the soul does not have a place to go. It cannot return to the body because the body has been destroyed and it cannot be let in to any of the worlds destined for the soul because its time has not yet come. Therefore, the soul is in a state of limbo, which is believed to be very painful (Kaplan & Shoenberg, 1988).

Conversely, Sarah has a strong religious foundation that she claims is her source of strength during her time of grief. She believes "...it's not to fear death, but to look forward to returning to God because that's where you came from". Muslims typically believe that death is not the end of an individual's life; death is a transition into a new phase of existence (Spiro, Curnen, & Wandel, 1996). Sarah's nine-year-old son Joseph also has a strong religious foundation. As part of the Muslim faith, they pray five times a day. Prayer is a time for direct connection with God and formal prayers are meant to constantly remind Muslims of the purpose of life and reaffirm their faith in God (Dodge, 2009). During one of these prayers Joseph says:

> When we say a prayer, it's different from prayer in the Western sense. Prayer in the Western sense is, "Oh God, give me this or do this." To that type prayer we call supplication....There are certain supplications he does and verses from the Quran that he reads which is like giving a gift to his [deceased father]...we believe God gives that person, their soul, that message....He has chosen a particular time of the day, every day, when he says his special prayer. It's his routine and it is his way of remembering his dad.

The word *du'a'* or *supplication* means "to call upon" God. Supplications are used to voice one's personal feelings and situation to God; it is a personal prayer to God asking for what you want (Chittick, 1992). Even before they go to sleep, the family reads a supplication. Sarah explained:

> ...[T]he basic meaning from Arabic is that from God we have come and we will return to him in a state of death when we sleep, but when we wake up in the morning and we read certain prayers praising Allah, praising God, that he has revived you from a state of death.

Mainstream Western culture tends to focus on the individual rather than the collective, to deny the importance of continuing bonds, and to identify abnormal grief reactions as pathological (Shapiro, 1996). Grieving individuals are expected to display certain emotional reactions, usually in the form of sadness and depression, over a typical length of time in order to grieve acceptably. These responses to death are considered the norm and reactions that are different from the norm are considered pathological or inappropriate. However, ethnic/minority families may have different norms (Webb, 2010). As a result, ethnic/minority children, and their families may experience *disenfranchised grief* when their cultural beliefs and practices are not recognized or respected by the majority culture (Webb, 2010, p. 96).

There are many similarities and differences across and within cultures and religions with respect to death, and it is important for educators to understand those differences, specifically the role of children in death rituals, in order to provide bereaved children with adequate support.

CHRISTIANITY

Christianity is considered a global religion, as it is adaptable to an enormous variety of cultural and social settings. At its most basic, Christianity focuses on the figure of Jesus Christ. Christianity is more than a system of religious beliefs. It has also generated a culture and practices, a set of ideas and ways of life, and artifacts that have been handed down generations since Jesus first became of the object of faith (Hick, 1994; Hale, 2010).
At the heart of Christianity lies the belief in an eternal life after death. Christians believe that dying is the end of a person's physical presence on Earth, but that the soul lives on in an afterlife. Christians believe that after death, a person's soul is faced with the presence of God and he judges them for the deeds they have done or failed to do during their lifetime. Those who reject God are sent to hell, a place of eternal fire, symbolizing pain and suffering. Those who are offered redemption and reconciliation with God, referred to as salvation, will spend eternity rewarded in Heaven (Hick, 1994; Hale, 2010).
The Christian funeral has three goals. The first is to reflect on the person's life on Earth. The second is to pray to God that the loved one enter Heaven. The third is to give strength to friends and family who are grieving the loss. A funeral is typically held a week after the time of death, following a one to two day wake or viewing. It is customary for family and friends to attend the wake or viewing in order to say goodbye to the deceased and to offer condolences to the family. Funerals are held in a church and led by a minister or a priest. The service is typically followed by a burial (Hick, 1994; Hale, 2010).

JUDAISM

The term Jewish refers to the culture, religion, history, and philosophy of life shared by a grouping of people whose origins trace back to the prophet Abraham. Judaism refers to the group of Jewish practitioner's religious beliefs (Rosdahl & Kowalski, 2008). Jewish practitioners believe that God created the world and humans were created in His image (Guzzetta, 1998). The Jewish faith has deep-rooted beliefs about life and death. The focus of the Jewish faith is on life and its preservation, and on establishing religion in people on earth rather than focusing on a world beyond this. Death is considered inevitable and natural because it comes from God and should not be feared (Guzzetta, 1998).

The idea of a soul is also a fundamental belief in Judaism. The soul is eternal; it comes from God and it precedes the existence of a human body. The soul is made up of five basic elements that are subdivided into more elements. The lowest soul is nefesh, and it is the soul's most physical aspect. In ascending order, the soul's other, more spiritual, elements are ruach, neshama, chayah, and yechidah. After death, the soul desires to leave the physical body and return to God. If the person has led a spiritual life, the desire to leave the body will be fulfilled. However, if the person focused on the material aspect of the world, the soul may remain rooted to the body. To what extent it reaches its spiritual destination depends on how one lives his or her life (Bank & Wiggins, 2005).

Jewish death practices help the bereaved to realize that their loved one is dead and to gradually fill that void (Matzo & Sherman, 2010). When a Jewish practitioner dies, the body should be treated with utmost respect. The limbs must be straightened, eyes must be closed, the lower jaw must be bound, and the body must be covered (Guzzetta, 1998). The body is then either buried or cremated; however if the person chooses to be cremated, his or her ashes cannot be buried in a Jewish cemetery (Matzo & Sherman, 2010).

Mourning rituals are meant to strengthen and support the family and honour the dead. The memory of the deceased during the mourning period must be maintained and carried on (Matzo & Sherman, 2010). The first period of mourning is called shiva which is commemorated by the wearing of a torn black ribbon (Guzzetta, 1998). Shiva refers to the seven days of intensive mourning beginning right after the funeral. During this week, the bereaved remain at home and friends and family visit to offer help and condolences. Family and friends also bring food to the mourning family so that they do not have to cook. The shiva candle burns for seven days and the family prepares a meal of comfort known as seudat havra'ah. Following shiva comes thirty days of sloshim. During shloshim, normal daily activities and events are resumed, but entertainment is avoided. If a parent dies, the mourning continues for an entire year (Matzo & Sherman, 2010).

HINDUISM

Hinduism is an umbrella term to describe a set of philosophies, cultures, and a way of life (Clements, Vigil, Manno & Henry, 2003). Hinduism does not have an institutional framework, or require an adherence to particular doctrines. Hinduism is a compilation of diverse beliefs and practices. Nevertheless, Hindu practitioners have specific beliefs in common that influence their attitudes to life and death. These beliefs relate to a transition to another life, whether by reincarnation, life in heaven with God, or absorption into Brahman, the ultimate reality (Firth, 2005). Many Hindu practitioners belong to traditions devoted to one God such as Krishna. They believe that those who are virtuous, with the Grace of God, will go to heaven and obtain liberation from

Samsara, the cycle of birth and death. Most Hindu practitioners believe there is a soul, or atma, in all living beings, which travels from one life to another. Hindu practitioners believe in karma and reincarnation which suggests that each birth is linked to actions taken in previous births. A belief in karma and reincarnation also suggests that births and deaths are part of a cycle where each person is seeking good karmas or actions, ultimately leading to Moksha or the liberation of the soul (Lobar, Youngblut & Brooten, 2006; Puchalski & O'Donnell, 2005). Of particular importance is the notion of a good death, which provides a model of how to die and a bad death, which is greatly feared (Firth, 2005). A good death involves selfless actions, void of any thought for its karma, and motivated by the love of God. Those who love God and think of Him at the time of death will meet Him in heaven (Firth 2005). Individuals live many lives until their souls, or atma, become one with God (Sharma, 1990).

When a Hindu practitioner dies, the body is bathed, massaged in oils, dressed in new clothes, and then cremated before the next sunrise. It is essential the body be cremated before the next sunrise because Hindu practitioners believe a person retains both a physical body and an astral body which houses the soul. It is believed that burying the body only encourages the soul to remain confused and earthbound (Clements, Vigil, Manno & Henry, 2003; Puchalski & O'Donnell, 2005). Death of a physical body does not mean death of the soul; therefore, immediate cremation is important to facilitate the soul's transition from this world to the next (Firth, 2005). Before the cremation occurs, the body is honoured. First, the oldest son offers water, incense, and flowers to the body. The oldest son is the primary agent in his parent's death rites; he will perform and orchestrate all the final rites. His performance of these rites will act as his final debt to his parent and assure the parent's safe passage to the realm of the ancestors. This is one of the main reasons why sons are valued so much more than daughters in the Hindu tradition (Garces-Foley, 2006). The death ritual then involves a procession to the cremation ceremony, placing the body on a pyre of wood, with the eldest son setting it aflame after repeating an ancient vedic prayer (Puchalski & O'Donnell, 2005). Once the body has been sufficiently burnt the son will take a stick and perform a final rite called kapak kriya, or *skull work*. This rite consists of cracking the skull of the dead parent in order to release the soul (Garces-Foley, 2006). The bones are then gathered and placed in a river with offerings, constructing the body for a new rebirth (Puchalski & O'Donnell, 2005). After cremation, the disembodied souls travel through various hells explaining their sins or they reside in temporary heavens (Firth, 2005).

Several rituals are observed over the next ten days, which are considered a time for prayer and meditation to help the departed soul's journey to the next world. It is believed that for these ten days, the soul remains watching over the house and releases its attachment to the former life on the eleventh day (Clements, Vigial, Manno & Henry, 2003; Lobar, Youngblut & Brooten, 2006). During this time, family members are in severe ritual impurity and live austerely; they eat only home-cooked meals once a day and they are not permitted to wash their clothes (Garces-Foley, 2006). On the eleventh day, the soul releases its attachment to the former life and on the twelfth day the family gathers with friends and community members to honour and remember the

Chapter Three: Cultural and Religious Aspects of Grieving

deceased (Clements, Vigial, Manno & Henry, 2003; Lobar, Youngblut & Brooten, 2006).

There is limited literature on the grieving process because Hinduism does not have an institutional framework nor demand an adherence to particular doctrines. According to Thakrar and Aery (2008), there is a specific period of purification and mourning following the death of a Hindu practitioner. This period generally lasts for thirteen days, though there is some variation according to family tradition and background. This is a period for social support, family bonding, and expression of grief (Thakrar & Aery, 2008). This period of purification and mourning starts immediately after the son cracks the parent's skull. This rite marks the beginning of the difficult work of forgetting. From this moment, relatives are supposed to leave grief and tears behind, as those only attract the soul back to this world (Garces-Foley, 2006). Each evening after this rite during the thirteen-day period, family members gather for prayers and meditation on behalf of the deceased individual. Because they are considered temporarily impure, they may not be allowed in the temple or to perform rituals. On the thirteenth day, a ceremony ends the official period of purification and mourning. After this date the bereaved family members are more susceptible to isolation, often making bereavement reactions more pronounced (Thakrar & Aery, 2008).

BUDDHISM

Buddhist Wheel of Life

Source: Wikimedia Commons

Buddhist practitioners view human life as a cycle of birth, death, and rebirth. They believe the cycle of life is driven by the law of karma, specifically the law of action. It is the law of karma that determines the quality of rebirth. Karma refers to good or bad actions a person takes during his or her lifetime. Good actions, such as generosity, righteousness, and meditation, bring about happiness. Bad actions, such as lying, stealing, or killing leads to unhappiness (Wada & Park, 2009). There are thirty-

Childhood Loss and Grief

one planes of existence into which any living being can be reborn, depending on his or her karma. The realm of man is considered the highest realm of rebirth because this realm offers an opportunity to achieve enlightenment, or nirvana (Mahathera, 2001). Buddhists practitioners can achieve nirvana by following the model of the Buddha. The Buddha is a representation of the Buddhist religion. The Buddha is not viewed as a powerful divinity that Buddhist practitioners need to worship as a god; rather, his followers see his life as a model for people to follow (Puchalski & O'Donnell, 2005). The Buddha is an *awakened* being, a symbolic figure, and a spiritual teacher whose lessons guide the practitioners to the path of liberation (Wada & Park, 2009). If practitioners of Buddhism follow this path of liberation and practice meditation, they will reach the realm of man, achieve detachment, and attain a state of enlightenment or nirvana (Puchalski & O'Donnell, 2005).

Buddhist practitioners believe death is an opportunity for improvement in the next life (Keown, 2005; Lobar, Youngblut & Brooten, 2006). After death, the spirit remains and seeks attachment to a new body and new life. To enter death in a positive state of mind and surrounded by monks and family helps the deceased to become reborn on a higher level (Lobar, Youngblut & Brooten, 2006). In Tibet, the day of death is thought of as highly important. It is believed that as soon as death has taken place, the personality goes into a state of trance for four days. During this time, the person does not know he or she is dead. This period is called the First Bardo. It is believed that towards the end of the First Bardo the dead person will see a luminous light. If the deceased welcomes the radiance of the Clear Light the person can be reborn. If the deceased flees the light, he or she then becomes conscious that death has occurred. At this point, the Second Bardo begins. The person sees all that he or she has done or thought. While the deceased watches his or her thoughts and actions, the deceased feels as though he or she has a body. When the individual realizes he or she does not have a body the deceased longs to possess one again. The deceased individual then transitions into the Third Bardo, which is the state of seeking another birth. All previous thoughts and actions direct the person to choose new parents who will give him or her a new body (Keown, 2005).

Buddhism originated in India 2,500 years ago. Buddhism evolved into many different forms as it traveled south and east from India through different regions of Asia, absorbing the cultural and indigenous spiritual traditions of those regions.(Please move to the opening paragraph of section. According to Wada and Park (2009) Buddhism has continued to transform itself as it has become more prominent in North America in the past fifty years. As a result of this continuous transformation and the increase in Buddhist practitioners from different cultures and regions of the world, it is very difficult to describe Buddhist death rituals because there are various rituals practiced by the different forms of Buddhism.(Please edit and rephrase for clarity.)

According to Masao (1983) when a Buddhist practitioner dies in Japan, the body of the deceased is cleaned, the eyes are closed, the hands are clasped, and the face is covered in a white cloth. A funeral is held either in the home or in the temple and mourners are invited to pray for the deceased. The deceased is then cremated seven days after death. Cremation cannot occur before the seventh day because if the body is cremated before the consciousness has left the body, the person will be disturbed during the final stages of transition. The purpose of the Buddhist funeral is to separate the spirit of the deceased from the body, guiding the former to the next life (Masao, 1983). Japanese culture has many folk beliefs about the deceased as dangerous wandering spirits. Shirei, or *newly dead*, can be translated as *ghost*, in the sense of *spook*. Until the deceased are safely in the ancestor world, they may cause harm to the living. Part of the reason for the funeral rites is to ensure the dead do not remain as wandering spirits (Garces-Foley, 2006). On the third, seventh, forty-ninth, and hundredth day after the death, a religious service is performed for the deceased. The forty-ninth day is particularly important because it marks the end of mourning (Masao, 1983).

During the forty-nine days after death, the relationship between the living and the dead is resolved. All human relationships entail unresolved conflict; therefore, it is very common for the deceased individual to return in a dream and say, "It's okay. You did your best" (Garces-Foley, 2006, p. 84). In other words, the dead forgive or say the relationship is now resolute. If a dream does not occur, the survivor may experience the feeling at some point during those forty-nine days that it is okay to let go of the deceased. When the survivor lets go of any ambivalence in the relationship, the deceased is free to go on and become an ancestor. If the relationship between the living and the dead is not resolved, the dead can become a harmful spirit or a hungry ghost, but this does not remain a permanent condition. The living and the dead are in continual interaction; therefore, reconciliation and the possibility of resolving relationships remains (Garces-Foley, 2006). Finally, one hundred days after an individual has died, a Buddhist ceremony is done in order to perform final prayers.

In Buddhism, the first principle of the Four Noble Truths states that life is suffering. Once one accepts this, he or she begins to understand that sickness, aging, and death are integral parts of the human experience. From the Buddhist perspective, suffering is temporary. Recognizing the temporary nature of suffering gives the bereaved strength to endure the pain or loss. From the Buddhist perspective, either severing the bond with the deceased or rigidly holding on to the loss will not lead one to cope with the loss in a wholesome way. Grief is about recognizing and honouring a changing bond with the deceased, while mindfully attending to the emotions of grief. Grief is often not addressed in contemporary Buddhism because a "good Buddhist" accepts death and releases the deceased (Roshi, 2006, p. 260). As noted above, the forty-ninth day after the death marks the end of the mourning period; as a result, Buddhist practitioners are expected to return to the life they lived before the death occurred (Wada & Park, 2009).

ISLAM

The central belief in the Muslim religion is that there is only one God known as *Allah* and *Muhammed* is God's prophet (Lobar, Youngblut & Brooten, 2006; Puchalski & O'Donnell, 2005). The word *Islam* means submission to and obeying the will of Allah (Koenig & Shohaib, 2014). There are five core beliefs (pillars) of Islam and they are the basis for Muslim life. They are "(1) the creed of belief (shahada), (2) daily prayers (salah), (3) giving to the poor (zakat), (4) fasting during Ramadan (sawm), and (5) pilgrimage to Mecca (hajj)" (Koenig & Shohaib, 2014, p. 28). In Islam, life is viewed as a test and whatever calamity befalls someone (disease, loss, etc.) they are not to question it because Muslims believe in destiny, "which means that everything—all events and happenings in life—have a purpose and there are no random occurrences" (Koenig & Shohaib, 2014, p. 32).

For Muslim practitioners, death marks the transition from one state of existence to the next; the earthly world is a test and a path to the next world and Muslim practitioners are encouraged to do good so as to prepare for the next world (Puchalski & O'Donnell, 2005; Sheikh, 1998). Rahman mentions that the life after death is "as concrete and palpable as the life in this world; there is a natural continuity between the two, and death is the passage between them" (Koenig & Shohaib, 2014, p. 33). Muslim practitioners believe that "the quality of life after death—either heaven or hell—is determined by an individual's performance during this life" (Koenig & Shohaib, 2014, p. 33). At the time of death, the soul (al ruh or al nafs meaning 'self') is separated from the soulless body (Miller, Ziad-Miller & Elamin, 2014). The soul rises to heaven, temporarily, and returns to the body when the deceased is buried (Spiro, Curnen & Wandel, 1996).

Following death, the Angel of Death removes the soul from the body. The goal of the journey of life is to reach a vision of God. Upon burial, the soul is returned to the grave and the deceased is visited in the grave for questioning; the deceased is determined to be a believer or an unbeliever. The believers are those who live righteous lives on earth and unbelievers are those who reject the teachings of Muhammed and live lives of sin on earth. On the Day of Resurrection, the dead will rise from their graves to await resurrection. Disbelievers and wrongdoers are chained together and forced to hell where they are punished for their sins, while believers are destined to inherit paradise through a second birth or resurrection. Those judged to be *spiritually advanced* are called "foremost in Faith" and are destined to spend eternity "nearest to God" (Ross, 2001, p. 84).

The Islamic tradition prescribes four Muslim funerary practices; ritual bathing of the corpse, shrouding, funeral prayer, and burial (Garces-Foley, 2006). Generally, Muslim practitioners are buried as soon as possible, preferably within twenty-four hours after death (Sheikh, 1998). In Islam, a burial represents the human being's return to the most elemental state, since the Creator formed humans from earthly materials; as a result, cremation is unacceptable because it is described as "the punishment of hell" (Komaromy, 2004, p. 33). Before a burial, family members of the same sex as the deceased prepare the deceased body by shutting the eyes and mouth, straightening and tying the limbs together, washing and wrapping the body in plain white linen and placing it in a wooden casket lying flat on his or her back (Lobar, Youngblut & Brooten, 2006; Mehraby, 2003; Sheikh, 1998). The deceased (within the casket) is then brought to a local mosque for funeral prayer. After the funeral prayer, all family and community members present at the time of funeral prayer follow the funeral procession to the graveyard. Although contrary to the religion, in some countries, Muslim women are not permitted to attend the burial, mainly due to the cultural belief that women are of 'faint heart' and will break down easily (Mehraby, 2003; Ross, 2001).

At the graveyard, the final prayer is said and the deceased is placed in its grave on its side facing Mecca (Sheikh, 1998). After the burial, two angels visit the deceased in the grave. The angels test the deceased on his or her faith and they "question [them] about [their] deeds in life" (Spiro et al., 1996, p.150). Individuals with good deeds and strong faith will pass this test and "may be relieved of the oppressiveness of the grave by the opening of a window to heaven through which refreshing breezes waft and comfort them" (Spiro et al., 1996, p.150). However, the wrongdoers and sinful individuals will face the punishment of grave and after the punishment the person remains unconscious until The Day of Resurrection (Spiro et al., 1996,). Muslim practitioners believe that there is going to be an end to this world and the day after the end of this world is called The Day of Resurrection. On this day, it is believed that "God will resurrect everyone (all those that have been in this world), even the dead will rise from their graves to await for resurrection, and those that have denied God's truth and gone astray in this world will suffer in the hell fire" (Koenig & Shohaib, 2014, p. 31; Ross, 2001). Whereas those that have submitted to God and have done good deeds in this world will be rewarded with an eternal life of happiness in heaven (Koenig & Shohaib, 2014).

Muslim practitioners believe that all suffering, life, death, joy, and happiness are created by Allah and that Allah provides strength to survive. These beliefs are usually sources of comfort and strength that aid the healing process. When a Muslim practitioner dies, it is permissible to cry and express grief over the death of a loved one; however, extreme weeping is discouraged. Although a grieving person may be compelled to express grief and sadness when crying over a deceased person, wailing and expressions of dissatisfaction with the decree of God is not welcomed. Individuals are encouraged to talk about and remember their loved one and recall the good deeds of their life. Quiet weeping with grief is allowed for however long it takes for the individual to readjust their life without the deceased; however, loud wailing is not permitted for longer than three days after the loss. This is because Muslims believe in destiny, and a lengthened exaggerated outward expression of the loss is believed to be going against the will of God (Ahmad, 1996). Muslim practitioners believe that death is inevitable and Allah appoints a time for each person to pass from this existence into the next.

CHAPTER 4

The Death of a Parent

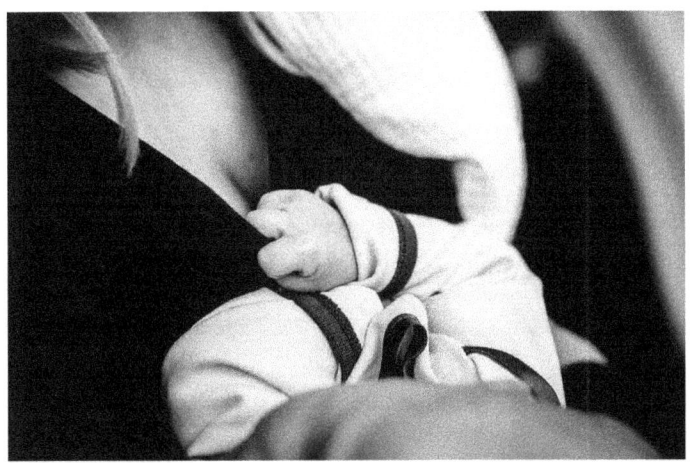

Source: Creative Commons

"I will never forget the moment your heart stopped and mine kept beating."
-Angela Miller

Childhood Loss and Grief

The death of a parent is likely the most difficult loss that a child can experience because parents are the most important people in a child's life (Silverman, 2000). For the vast majority of children, parents remain the most significant others. Parents typically support their children, both physically and emotionally; parents provide a secure home environment in which children can grow and mature; and parents act both as the children's protectors and as their models (Worden, 1996). Immediately after birth, infants begin to develop an attachment to their parents, promoting social and emotional development. Parental responses to this relationship lead to the development of attachment, which further supports the development of the child's emotions, thoughts, and feelings (Silverman, 2000). Essentially, parents are negotiating the necessary developmental tasks that will lead children to adulthood (Worden, 1996). When a parent dies, the child loses a key relationship; thus, creating profound change in the child's social, emotional, and cognitive capacity. The child loses a significant person in his or her life, as well as the sense of security that existed in that relationship (Silverman, 2000). The loss of a parent to death and the effects the parent's death has in the home and in the family, changes the very heart of the child's existence (Worden, 1996).

Category	Responses
Physical	• Difficulty breathing, fatigue, muscle weakness, stomach aches, head aches • Increased susceptibility to disease. Thoughts affect nervous system which impacts immune system • Fill the hole/void by eating, excessive activity/exercise, playing video games, watching TV
Emotional	• Mental health difficulties: increased risk of developing psychatric disorders and may trigger psychological and social difficulties • Denial, panic attacks, high anxiety, fear of abandonment and separation
Cognitive	• Difficulty understanding death • Repeatedly asking questions about death • Decrease in academic performance
Behavioural	• Regressive behaviour, feeling insecure, bed wetting, need to co-sleep, reverting to babbling

Source: Merenda

GENERAL DEVELOPMENTAL RESPONSES TO BEREAVEMENT

Children are impacted by bereavement in physical, social, emotional, and cognitive ways. The following are general developmental responses to bereavement. Although there are general responses to bereavement, recognizing how the death of a parent affects children across all developmental domains requires examination of several influencing factors.

DEVELOPMENTAL PROCESSES

A child's age has a significant impact on his or her adjustment to the loss of a parent. Children of different ages are working through different developmental tasks and the death of a parent will almost certainly affect the way in which a child negotiates those tasks (Worden, 1996). Children at each age grieve differently and some researchers suggest children's mourning is brief and intermittent, re-emerging in different ways at each developmental level (Nickman, Silverman, & Normand, 1998; Speece, & Brent, 1984). Children in all age groups may develop severe depressive and somatic symptoms and some age groups have been found to be at greater risk for maladaptation. Research suggests that children who are younger than five years of age appear to be more vulnerable to later adjustment problems and adolescent or adult mental illness (Christ, 2000; Hunter, & Smith, 2008; Lehman, Lang, Wortman, & Sorenson, 1989; McGuinness, 2011); however, longitudinal research that observes grieving children over a period of time is very limited. In order for researchers to understand how the death of a parent affects children in adulthood, it is necessary for research to look at the grieving processes of children in their environments over time (Stroebe, Hansson, Stroebe, & Schut, 2001).

Cognitive Development

Piaget theorized predictable stages of cognitive development that occur during specific periods of a child's life. The development of these stages is contingent upon the child's interactions with his or her environment. According to Piaget, children's cognitive abilities progress through four stages that allow for maturation of children's ability to think and process information. Although Piaget's theory of cognitive development does not specifically address children's conceptualizations of loss, understanding Piaget's theory is fundamental in recognizing how children might perceive and respond to grief.

Children's understanding of death does not exist in isolation from other developments taking place in their cognitive life. Children require a certain level of understanding and maturity when it comes to comprehending death; their level of maturity is related to their age, life experiences, and cognitive development (Heath et al., 2008). A child's conceptualization of death varies with overall level of cognitive development (Hunter & Smith, 2008). According to Speece and Brent (1984), several cognitive achievements are essential for children's ability to understand death. These cognitive achievements include a linear notion of time; an ability to perform reversible operations; an ability to learn from experiences of others; and an increase in objectivity and decreased egocentrism.

Piaget's Four Stages of Cognitive Development

Age Range	Stage	Characteristics
0-2 Years	Sensorimotor	<ul><li>Children understand and make sense of their world through sensory and motor exploration</li><li>Development of object permanence and symbolic thought</li></ul>
2-7 Years	Preoperational	<ul><li>Pre-conceptual (2-4): immature use of concepts</li><li>Intuitive thought (4-7): egocentric</li></ul>
7-11 Years	Concrete Operations	<ul><li>Transition from pre-logical thinking to thinking with logic</li><li>Thinking is concrete</li><li>Understands conservation, reversibility, classification</li></ul>
12 + Years	Formal Operations	<ul><li>Increased ability to use logic</li><li>Abstract thinking</li><li>Deductive reasoning</li></ul>

Adapted from Burns, 2010

It is not until children are between five and seven years of age that they develop an understanding for irreversibility, non-functionality, universality, and inevitability (Dyregrov, 2008). According to Speece and Brent (1984), irreversibility is an understanding that once a living thing dies, its physical body cannot be made alive again; **non-functionality** is an understanding that all life-defining functions end at death; and **universality** is knowledge that all living things die. According to Hunter and Smith (2008) **inevitability** is a comprehension that one cannot control death. Once children understand these components of death they are able to acknowledge the deceased parent has not abandoned them, which in turn will positively influence their grieving process.

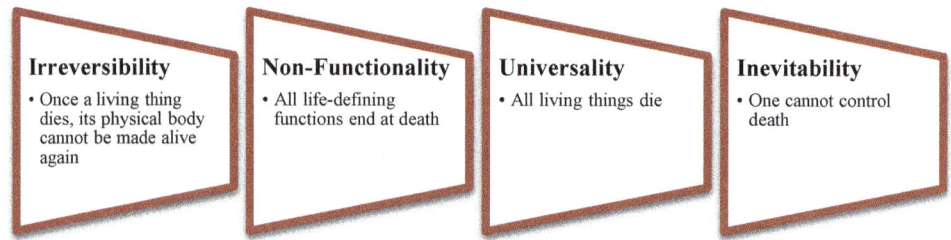

Source: Merenda

The ability to conceptualize more abstract aspects of death coincides with Piaget's Cognitive Theory beginning with the *preoperational stage*. Children believe that death is temporary and reversible, and they relate death to concrete observations such as the deceased's closed eyes (Slaughter, 2005). They believe the deceased parent can return after receiving medical intervention, after eating and drinking water, by magic, through wishful thinking, and by praying (Speece & Brent, 1984). During the *concrete operational stage*, children understand that the deceased is gone permanently but they still do not understand that death as something that occurs from outside of the body. Finally, in the *formal operational stage*, the child understands the finality, the biology and the irreversibility of death (Slaughter, 2005).

COGNITIVE ACHIEVEMENTS REQUIRED FOR CHILDREN'S ABILITY TO UNDERSTAND DEATH

Consistent with Piaget's stages of cognitive development is the work of Maria Nagy. In 1984, Nagy conducted interviews with 378 Hungarian children between three and ten years old. All of the children were asked questions about death and children between the ages of six and ten were asked to create drawings depicting their ideas about death. Based on the interview, Nagy developed one of the earliest models of children's understanding of death (Burns, 2010)

Nagy's Stages of a Child's Understanding of Death

Stage	Age	Description
Stage One	3-5 Years	Children see death as a departure from a place. The person who died has moved and is living else where.
Stage Two	5-9 Years	Children believe that death may be avoided.
Stage Three	9-10 Years	Children understand that death is permanent, inevitable, and affects all living things.

Source: Merenda

Psychosocial Development

Erik Erikson theorized that social and emotional development continues across the lifespan. He developed eight stages of psychosocial development, with a central issue requiring resolution at the core of each stage. Successful resolution of the conflict results in healthy development (Burns, 2010).

The first four stages are specific to children's development. Although the conflicts in each stage are based on predictable or normative experiences, death (non-normative events) can result in a negative resolution at any stage. For example, in looking at the stage of ***Initiative vs. Guilt***, children might feel guilty over their parent's death because children believe that they were responsible for the death. This guilt might occur because the line between reality and fantasy are blurred in part because of magical thinking. ***Magical thinking*** is the belief children have that they can make things happen with their thoughts and wishes.

Erikson's Eight Stages of Psychosocial Development
Adapted from Burns, 2010

Age Range	**Psychosocial Stage**	**Characteristics**
0-18 Months	Trust vs. Mistrust	• Trust built through nurturing relationships with caregivers • Mistrust developed by neglectful and inconsistent caregiving
1 ½ - 3 Years	Autonomy vs. Shame and Doubt	• Autonomy develops as toddlers master skills such as walking and toileting. • Feelings of shame and doubt arise when toddlers fail to master skills
3-6 Years	Initiative vs. Guilt	• Children take initiative in their actions, even if the actions are beyond their abilities • Inability to sustain initiatives can create conflict with caregivers and result in guilt for children.
6-12 Years	Industry vs. Inferiority	• Industriousness and competency develop through mastery of academic and social skills • Feelings of inferiority develop as a result of failure to achieve these skills
12-18 Years	Identity vs. Role Confusion	• Adolescents grapple with the resolution of personal, social, and occupational identity issues • Failure to resolve the issues can lead to confusion in adulthood
Young Adulthood	Intimacy vs. Isolation	• Inability to form intimate friendships and relationships can create feelings of isolation and loneliness
Middle Adulthood	Generativity vs. Stagnation	• Productivity of self and others results in sense of generativity. • Non-productivity results in stagnancy
Older Adulthood	Integrity vs. Despair	• Integrity is established when the older adult looks back on life with a sense of fulfillment • Unfulfilled goals result in a sense of despair

Chapter Four: The Death of a Parent

Source: Merenda

Ecological Systems Theory

Urie Bronfenbrenner's ecological systems theory explores the influence of interacting social systems on children's development. The connectedness and relationships among the multiple social systems affect every aspect of a child's development. The following figure depicts the multiple social systems and the people or places involved in each system.

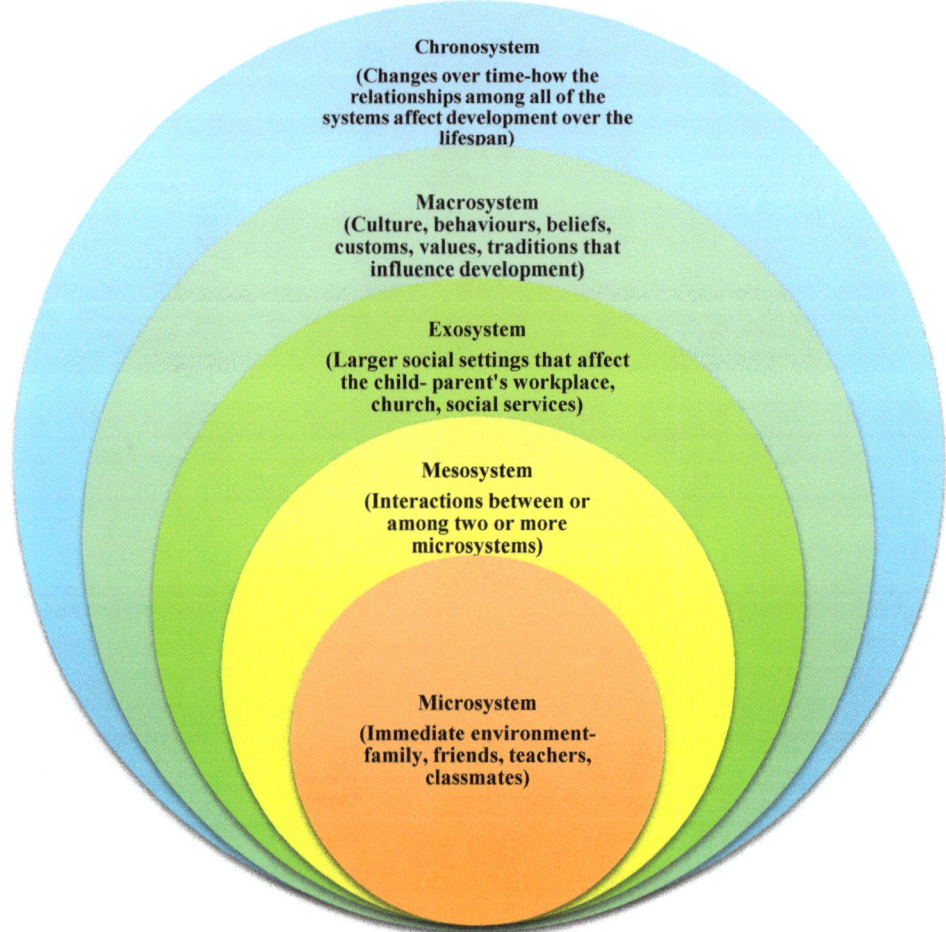

Source: Merenda

CHILDREN'S AGE AS A PREDICTOR FOR RESPONSE TO THE DEATH OF A PARENT

Miraglia (2012) conducted research on how the death of a parent effects children. Her research included interviews with a bereavement counsellor and two remaining parents, Mike and Sarah. Like (Worden, 1996), Miraglia's (2012) research revealed that children of different ages are struggling with different developmental tasks and ultimately, the death of a parent will affect the way in which a child works through those tasks. The bereavement counsellor explained that the death of a parent affects children across all developmental levels and ages:

> Children are like barometers; they sense every change in the atmosphere... [C]hildren as young as eighteen months will sense something is different...For really young kids who can't really understand the idea of death, can't have a conversation about it, can't have it be explained to them...you will still see the effects on their behaviour.

She explained that a set timeline for grief does not exist and children are going to grieve the death of a parent throughout their life. Children's understanding of death does not exist independently from other developments taking place in their life (Miraglia, 2012). This echoes the work of many, who argue that a child's conceptualization of death varies with overall levels of cognitive development (Christ, 2000; Hunter & Smith, 2008; Lehman, Lang, Wortman, & Sorenson, 1989, Nickman, Silverman, & Normand, 1998; Speece & Brant, 1984; Webb, 2010).

The bereavement counsellor underscored the fact that at each stage of development, children's understanding of death matures, and along with this maturation comes curiosity and query. Interestingly, both parent participants expressed their experiences with their children's curiosity, query, and fear of death and an afterlife. For example, one parent said: "...[T]he immediate changes were, they were very worried that something was going to happen to them, that something was going to happen to me".

Parents reiterated that their children believe that the people they love will never die. Parents often reassure their children that they will always be there to care for them. This desire parents have to shield their children from death is understandable; however, when a death directly affects children, children can no longer be protected from the reality of death (Schonfeld & Quackenbush, 2009). When a parent dies, children typically fear the other parent will also die, especially if the remaining parent becomes ill. Children may believe that all illnesses have the same outcome (Curie, 2008). As a result, remaining parents should help their children understand that death is a part of life because the more parents try to shield their children, the more confusing and frightening death can be for children (Lasher, 2008). The bereavement counsellor suggested that parents worry that as soon as they talk about the possibility of their own death with their children, parents are taking away their children's hope; however, children can have information and still have hope.

On more than one occasion, Mike's oldest daughter Laura, who was five years old when her mom died, has spoken to Mike about her fear of her own mortality. Her fear is that this is the only life she will have the opportunity to live. "When I ask, 'what do you mean'...she says...'that I am going to live my life and then that's it'". Her fear is not that she is going to die; rather, Mike believes Laura's fear is that an afterlife does not exist: "It's more of an esoteric worry for her and I don't think it's like, 'I am worried I am going to die'. It's more like, 'what's next?'"

Sarah experienced a very similar conversation with her four-year-old child, Maggie, who asks questions about the possibility of other family members dying, as well as the possibility of her own death. Sarah provided a detailed plan for her children in the event of her death. "... [W]ell, I said, 'likely nana will be there and Dede', my sister, 'knows she is responsible for you guys if something happens to mommy and daddy'. I said things to reassure them". It is important to be honest when talking to children about death, especially during times of grief. When children question what will happen to them in the event both parents die, the remaining parent should provide information in a way as to prepare children for an unexpected death (Corr & Balk, 2010). The bereavement counsellor explained that when someone dies in a child's life, the world seems confusing and out of control. All the child wants during this time of upheaval is to know what they can count on as being consistent. The bereavement counsellor states:

> ...When a child asks the [remaining] parent, 'What if you die?' So many parents want to ease their child's fear and they say, 'I am not going to'. Well, that other parent wasn't supposed to either and the fact that they did made the fact that people die a true reality in the child's world, and so a parent saying, 'I am not going to die' is not going to bring any comfort to that child.

Explaining to children what their life will look like should both parents die, provides children with comfort and control because the children will know what to expect.

The following section summarizes how children of different ages are believed to be affected by the death of a parent and how they express their grief.

Birth to Three Years Old

Infants do not have the cognitive capability to understand an abstract concept like death (Fiorelli, 2002); however, Bowlby theorized that infants at approximately six to eight months of age are capable of grief because they develop a sense of *object permanence* (the understanding that objects exist even when they cannot be observed) with the caregiver (Christ, 2000). If the caregiver does not return after repeated protests over time, despair develops, eventually leading to detachment. Attachment disorders often develop, and can slow social, emotional, and cognitive development (Pomeroy & Garcia, 2009). For an infant, the most painful emotions associated with grief may include intense feelings of abandonment and disruptions in forming future healthy attachments with others (Pomeroy & Garcia, 2009; Lehman, Lang, Wortman, & Sorenson, 1989).

Johnson (1999) and Willis (2002) acknowledge that infants respond to the changes in the schedule, the tension he or she feels in his or her remaining parent, and to the disruption in the home. Furthermore, Geis et al. (1998) states that children between six months and one year can maintain *object constancy*, the internal representation of their parent, even when this parent is absent; therefore, leading to the conclusion that even children as young as infancy can experience an emotional reaction following the death of a parent. This present research later confirms the belief that children as early as infancy have the ability to grieve the death of a parent.

A toddler may express grief by regressing back to a younger stage of development when the family was in a safer and happier time, before the death of the parent (Kirwin & Hamrin, 2005). This regression usually presents itself as thumb sucking and toileting accidents (Christ, 2000). Toddlers also display separation anxiety, clinginess, and tantrums, along with obvious feelings of sadness and withdrawal. A grieving toddler may be afraid of the dark and they often experience sleep disturbances and nightmares. Toddlers frequently feel they have caused the sadness and grief they sense in others around them and lack the necessary verbal skills to understand that this is not the case (McGuinness, 2011).

Three to Five Years Old

Children of this age are believed to be in the pre-operational stage of their development and thus lack the cognitive ability to understand death (Boyd, Johnson, & Bee, 2012). Children do not yet understand concrete logic, cannot mentally manipulate information, and are unable to understand other's perspectives. These pre-operational cognitive attributes make it difficult for children to understand the meaning and the permanence of death (Hunter, & Smith, 2008). Since children at this stage do not understand death, they are more likely to express their grief with irritability, regression, stomach aches, and repetitious questions (McGuinness, 2011). Similar to infants, children of this age range experience intense separation anxiety because they are learning to trust and form basic attachments (Fiorelli, 2002); however, unlike infants, children in this stage are able to express their thoughts and feelings through play, fantasy, and drawings (Christ, 2000). Children of this age often engage in magical thinking and believe that their thoughts or behaviours caused their parent's death (Pomeroy & Garcia, 2009).

Six to Eight Years Old

Children in this age range have an advantage over younger children because they possess more advanced language skills. This group of children are most able to speak openly about death, because younger children cannot and often, older children will not (Hunter, & Smith, 2008). Children of this age range demonstrate sadness and anger over their loss and often experience physical symptoms such as stomach aches in response to their grief (McGuinness, 2011). They often experience fearfulness, sleeping problems, and separation anxiety. Moreover, finding a place for the deceased parent, like heaven where the parent is watching them, is very common. Children's late pre-operational cognitive capacities influence magical thinking about the causes of death which may lead to feelings of guilt and self-blame (Christ, 2000). Children may develop fears associated with their own death or the death of the remaining parent (Pomeroy & Garcia, 2009).

Nine to Twelve Years Old

Children at this age understand that death is final and it in inevitable for everyone. They recognize that death leads to changes in a family and they cannot control these changes. They worry about their remaining parent dying and these fears are heightened by the physical and hormonal changes occurring in their own bodies. Children at this stage may feel very vulnerable due to the need to blend in with their peers. Death can make them feel different and socially isolated (Pomeroy & Garcia, 2009). Therefore, children of this age need detailed, factual information about their parents' death in order to gain some sense of control over the event. They often express their feelings by being messy, stubborn, argumentative, and withdrawn (Christ, 2000). Children in this age range may control their grief by compartmentalizing; they refrain from talking about their loss or the emotions as a result of their loss (Lehman, Lang, Wortman, & Sorenson, 1989).

AGE AS A PREDICTOR FOR HOW CHILDREN RESPOND TO THE DEATH OF A PARENT

Birth-3 Years	3-5 Years	6-8 Years	9-12 Years
• Lack cognitive ability to understand death • Develop sense of object permanence; therefore, capable of grief • Repeated protest without comfort leads to detachment from caregiver • Feelings of abandonment and disruptions in forming future healthy attachments • **Expressions of Grief:** regression, thumb sucking, bed wetting, tantrums, clinginess, separation anxiety	• Pre-operational stage of development; therfore, lack the cognitive abilty to understand death • Do not understand concrete knowledge and unable to take on the point of view of other people • Difficulties understanding the meaning and permanence of death • Able to express thoughts through play • **Expressions of Grief:** irritable, regression, stomach aches, repetitive questions	• Understand death is final • Able to speak openly about death • Demonstrate sadness and anger over their loss • Imagining the parent in heaven is common • Pre-operational cognitive capacities influence magical thinking about the cause of death which lead to feelings of guilt and self-blame • **Expressions of Grief:** stomach aches, fearfulness, sleeping problems, and separation anxiety	• Understand death is final and inevitable • Feel vulnerable and different from their peers • Need detailed, factual information about their parent's death in order to gain control of the event • Control their grief by compartmentalizing • Don't talk about their loss or their emotions • **Expression of Grief:** messy, stubborn, argumentative, and withdrawn

Source: Merenda

ATTACHMENT AND RESPONSE TO THE DEATH OF A PARENT

Bowlby (1980) argued that attachment to a caregiver provides a safe base for infants and it assures protection and survival. Bowlby maintained that when the attachment figure is not available, infants and children will experience separation anxiety. He defined a sequence of emotional phases that infants experience when a caregiver is absent: protest (separation anxiety), despair (grief and mourning), and detachment (indifference) (Burns, 2010).

Mary Ainsworth conducted a study called the *Strange Situation*, which she developed to assess the quality of attachment between an infant and caregiver. The experiment was designed to measure children's sense of security and attachment. It involved babies and toddlers between the ages of ten and twenty-four months placed in various circumstances involving the presence or absence of the children's mother

Chapter Four: The Death of a Parent

or a stranger. Based on the child's response to the mother's return, Ainsworth identified three attachment styles: secure attachment, insecure-avoidant attachment, and insecure-resistant attachment. More recently, a fourth attachment style has been identified: insecure-disorganized attachment (Burns, 2010).

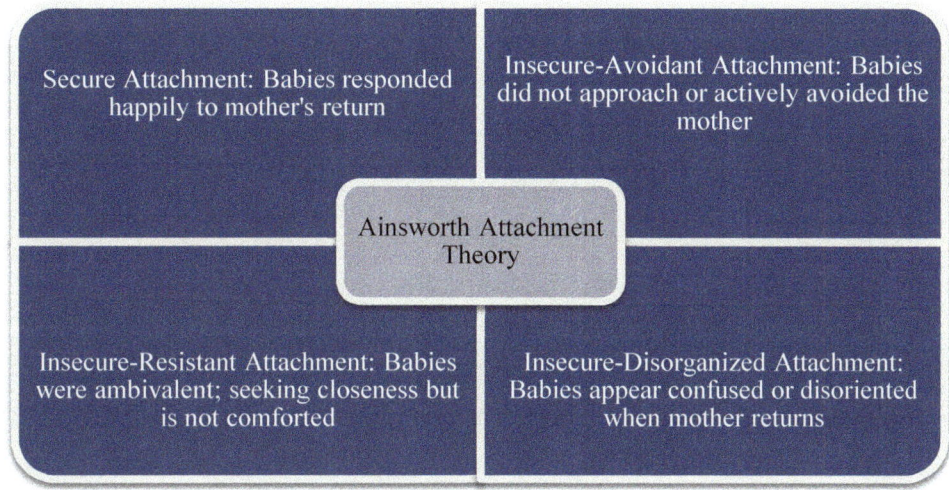

Source: Merenda

Parkes (2001) explains that attachment styles play an important role in children's reactions to loss. The way a child responds to loss depends on the child's relationship with the attachment figure (as cited in Burns, 2010).

Many studies have found attachment as a key factor moderating children's experience of stressful life situations (Charles & Charles, 2006). Threats, separation or permanent breaks in the attachment system can be very distressing and traumatic for children (Howell et al., 2016). A permanent physical separation from an attachment figure is the most difficult life adversity for a child because they lose their secure base and "must fortify other existing attachment relationships in response to that loss" (Howell et al., 2016, p. 153).

Furthermore, the death of an attachment figure "produces a cascade of secondary losses, including loss of the assumptive world, loss of essential caregiving behaviours, loss of proximity and comfort from the attachment figure, and loss of bio-behavioural regulation furnished by the attachment figure" (Howell et al., 2016, p. 153). Holmes (2014) states that experiencing bereavement during the early years (first five years) "can have long-lasting effects on the sensitivity of brain receptors, leading to permanently raised anxiety levels during the adult years" (p. 79).

Many studies suggest that attachment style has profound implications for the grief process, but it is not clear to what extent the quality of attachment may change as a result of the death of a parent (Charles & Charles, 2006). According to Miller (1971), children's reactions to loss usually have "a unique aim: to avoid the acceptance of the reality and emotional meaning of the death and to maintain in some internal form the relationship that has been ended" (as cited in Charles & Charles, 2006, p. 78). The experience of a loss may impede "a child's ability to develop new relationships by not allowing him or her to accept the loss or reinvest in new love objects" (Charles & Charles, 2006, p. 78).

Secure Attachment Style and Parental Loss

Holmes (2014) points out that children with *secure attachment style* "have the ability to tolerate both negative and positive emotions and to be overwhelmed by neither" (p. 79). In addition, Charles and Charles (2006) claim that children with secure attachment are found to better cope with trauma, such as a loss, and are better at enhancing their sense of self-efficacy; "[facilitating] the development of positive, constructive strategies for dealing with stressful situations, resulting in improved adjustment (Charles & Charles, 2006, p. 78). Thus, attachment styles greatly influence the coping mechanism children use during the process of a loss. (Charles & Charles, 2006).

According to Stroebe et al., parentally bereaved children with secure attachment styles are able to cope with grief better and "retain a range of bonds, physical and symbolic, as they are not driven by the need to reconnect physically with the deceased" (as cited in Maccallum & Bryant, 2013, p. 716). They are able to direct a greater allocation of mental effort towards metacognitive awareness (Noppe, 2000, p. 530). Children with secure attachment styles seek support in times of stress, "perhaps because secure individuals are more likely to expect others to be available as resources" (Charles & Charles, 2006, p. 78). Losing a caregiver is very painful; despite this, secure children are able to reinvest in a new life without the deceased, and maintain and/or modify their relationship to the lost attachment figure (Noppe, 200).

Insecure Attachment Styles (Avoidant, Resistant and Disorganized) and Parental Loss

Stroebe, Schut and Stroebe (2005) claim that children with *insecure-avoidant-*attachment *style* avoid grief work, those with *resistant-attachment style* experience relentless grief work, and those with *insecure-disorganized attachment* experience disturbed and incoherent grief work.

Children with insecure attachments are not able to direct an allocation of mental effort toward metacognitive monitoring because "the information [about their attachment figure] can be distorted, disorganized, and most especially, defended" (Noppe, 2000, p. 530). Noppe (2000) puts forth that: "A reworking of the representational relationship with the deceased attachment figure becomes more difficult when the memories are inaccessible, conflicted, or nonrepresentational. Perhaps it is here that the socially constructed biography within a supportive social context may help the bereaved child to continue the bond. Left unattended, the evolved well-organized defenses of infancy and childhood can lead to an entrenched defensive structure in dismissing or unresolved adults, who can close off their feelings when faced with loss and/or fail to engage in the cognitive restructuring of self as implied in the notion of reorganization in the mourning process" (p. 530). In addition, Maccallum and Bryant (2013) claim that bereaved children with insecure-resistant attachment tend to cling firmly to all types of bonds, in an attempt to regain physical proximity with the attachment figure.

CHILDREN'S GRIEF WORK AND ATTACHMENT STYLES

Attachment Style	Children's Grief Work
Secure Attachment	<ul><li>Are more likely to experience normal grief</li><li>Express their emotions at moderate levels</li><li>Seek support from others</li><li>Have higher chances of successful reinvestment in a new life without the deceased</li><li>Able to maintain a relationship with the lost attachment figure throughout their development</li></ul>
Insecure-Avoidant Attachment	<ul><li>Tend to avoid grief</li><li>Rarely express their emotions</li><li>Avoid seeking support</li><li>Are not able to maintain a relationship with the lost attachment figure throughout their development</li></ul>
Insecure-Resistant Attachment	<ul><li>Experience persistent grief work</li><li>Tend to strictly hold on to bonds with an attempt to regain physical proximity with the lost attachment figure</li><li>Engage in constant expression of heavy emotions,</li><li>Experience high levels of anxiety</li></ul>
Insecure-Disorganized Attachment	<ul><li>Experience disturbed and incoherent grief</li><li>Are highly challenged to express their emotions</li><li>Are not able to allocate a representational relationship with the lost attachment because information about their attachment figure is disorganized, inaccessible or nonrepresentational</li></ul>

Source: Merenda

Attachment relationships between a child and parent during childhood are the building blocks for emotional regulation, beliefs about the self and others, and a predictor to future relationships and romantic relationships during the adult years. Losing a parent during childhood leaves permanent life-long impacts. It may "affect the individual's ability to form and maintain the emotional ties necessary to sustain a relationship" (Høeg et al., 2018, p. 2). For example, when these children make new relationships, they are usually very cautious when establishing these relationships due to the fear of losing the person(s) they have established new relationships with (Høeg et al., 2018).

Research found that adults with avoidant or anxious attachment that had lost a parent during childhood, often report less satisfaction, intimacy, and trust in their relationships, thus increasing the risk of a breakup (Høeg et al., 2018). Results from one study showed that "bereaved children are more likely to develop insecure attachments as adults, adding to earlier evidence that adults who experienced early parental death showed less secure attachment styles in adulthood" (Høeg et al., 2018, p. 7). However, it is important to keep in mind that developmental pathways are complex and the links between parental loss, attachment, and relationship outcomes should not be oversimplified. The following table summarizes how children's grief work may look based on their attachment style with their primary caregivers.

GENDER AS A PREDICTOR FOR RESPONSE TO THE DEATH OF A PARENT

Research regarding predictors for how children respond to the death of a parent emphasizes gender as a factor in children's grief experience and adjustment (Lawhon, 2004; Raveis et al., 1999). Raveis et al. (1999) interviewed a group of children between three and eighteen months following the death of a parent from cancer. The researchers discovered that depressive symptoms were significantly related to a child's gender. Parentally bereaved girls reported higher levels of depressive symptoms than boys. Similarly, in their investigation of post-traumatic stress symptoms in parentally bereaved children, Stoppelbein and Greening (2000) concluded that parentally bereaved girls and younger children reported more post-traumatic stress disorder symptoms than boys and older children. Furthermore, Hope and Hodge (2006) reported that the male children they interviewed tended to externalize their grief and exhibit more acting out behaviour, whereas females tended to internalize their grief. The female participants were more verbal and expressive; they were better able to express their feelings verbally, but boys acted out their feelings in art or construction activities.

Worden (1996) states that parentally bereaved girls, regardless of their age, feel more anxious than boys during the first two years of grief. This anxiety manifests itself in concerns about the wellbeing of the remaining parent, as well as their own wellbeing. Girls are also socialized to be more sensitive than boys to family arguments that may occur in the early months after the death. Somatic symptoms are also more likely to be experienced by girls, especially during the first year after their parent's death. Furthermore, girls are more likely to speak to their remaining parent about the death, are more prone to cry throughout the first year of bereavement, and are more able to share their feelings with their family. Girls seem to be more attached to the deceased parent than boys and after the first year of grief, girls are more likely to idealize the deceased parent (Hope & Hodge, 2006).

Conversely, boys are more likely to evaluate their behaviour as inferior to their peers', and boys are more apt to have learning difficulties during their first year of bereavement. Stokes (2009) puts forth that "a boy may seem cheerful, playful and resilient but on the inside he may actually feel lonely, afraid, and desperate," (p.12) Due to the social pressure placed on them, boys are also more likely to be told they need to "grow up" and be the man of the house in the early months after the loss of a parent. Hope and Hodge (2006) conclude that parentally bereaved male and female children react and adjust to parental death differently due to differences in socialization. It is more acceptable for girls in the West to grieve openly than it is for boys. Furthermore, Hope and Hodge (2006) noted that male children seem to get more support if they show their grief because people do not expect them to react that way.

Gender Variations in Children's Responses to Parental Death

Female Children	Male Children
Girls tend to exhibit internalizing problems	Boys tend to exhibit externalizing problems
Girls display higher depressive and post-traumatic stress disorder symptoms	Boys are more likely to exhibit behavioural disturbances than girls (Lawrence, Jeglic, Matthews & Pepper, 2006)
Girls are better at expressing their feelings through communication	Boys are better at expressing their feelings through art or construction activities
Girls are more likely to experience somatic symptoms during the first year after their parent's death, and are likely to feel more anxious than boys during the first two years after their loss	Boys are more likely to experience learning difficulties during the first year after their parent's death
Socially, girls are taught to be more sensitive than boys; therefore, they are more likely to share their feelings and cry to others	Socially, boys are taught to act tough and keep their emotions to themselves, therefore they are more likely to hide their emotions and are less likely to communicate their feelings

Source: Merenda

This variation in grief reactions for boys and girls stems from the different ways in which boys and girls are socialized to express their feelings. Society establishes cultural norms around gender that impact how children grieve. Parents often socialize children differently when it comes to learning about death and grief. Society will often instill feminine and masculine ways of grieving, which impacts how children express and cope with grief. Commonly, boys are encouraged to be strong and refrain from expressing sadness; therefore, they often have more difficulty allowing themselves to express grief.

While girls are generally socialized to show sadness, they are often taught that anger and physical expression of that anger is inappropriate. Therefore, grief originated anger gets repressed (Wolfelt, 2010).

The differences in the ways boys and girls grieve may also be influenced by the differences in their play and friendships. Girls tend to play in pairs; their play is expressive; it centres around relationships; and through their play they develop the skills for using their language to express their feelings. Boys' play focuses on learning their role in the group and sticking to rules. Boys' play does not typically involve expression of feelings (Dyregrov, 2008).

GENDER MATCH AS A PREDICTOR FOR RESPONSE TO THE DEATH OF A PARENT

Worden (1996) credited differences in child behaviour following a parent's death to the gender of the deceased parent and, to some extent, to the gender of the child. All children need parental involvement and support, but boys and girls may look to each parent for the fulfillment of different needs. Children from Worden's (1996) study who had lost a same-gender parent were more likely to identify with the dead parent and to see themselves as more like that parent than the remaining one.

Gender mismatch also had a large influence on children's bereavement experiences. Children who lost a parent of the opposite gender felt more fear for the safety of the remaining parent and reported more health problems during the first year; however, gender mismatch had less influence during the second year of bereavement. Interestingly, girls who experienced mother loss had more emotional and behavioural problems at the first-year assessment (Worden, 1996).

Research shows that the loss of a mother is especially more difficult for children, than the loss of a father (Saler & Skolnick, 1992; Silverman & Worden, 1992). This distinction might be due to the fact that mothers are typically the primary caregivers and they are the more nurturing parent. It may also be because fathers often struggle to establish a warm, open, and caring climate in the house after the mother's death. Men typically have less experience from childhood in using language to support others during emotionally upset events, which would make it difficult for them to maintain a caring climate in the home. Furthermore, when a mother dies, girls often take on responsibility for more tasks in the home, in relation to male siblings and the father. This pressure to care for the home and the family can result in long-term negative consequences for female children (Dyregrov, 2008).

CAUSE OF DEATH AS A PREDICTOR FOR RESPONSE TO THE DEATH OF A PARENT

Researchers have not agreed on whether or not parent's cause of death has an impact on children's grief. In some studies, traumatic and sudden parental death was associated with post-traumatic stress disorder symptoms, increased risk for depressive disorder, and an increased risk for suicidal behaviour (Cerel, Jordan, & Duberstain, 200). However, the results of a study conducted by Brown (2007) involving children who lost a parent to a violent death, indicated that death caused by violence or suicide was not a major predictor of mental health problems in children and was not an indicator of bereaved children's need for intervention (as cited in Dave, Kissil, & Lynch, 2016).

Although more research is required to determine how the circumstances of a parent's death impacts children's adjustment to the loss, a summary of the current research findings for different types of death and the impact on children's grief is provided below.

Anticipatory and Unanticipated Death

Yearly, more than 3 million people die worldwide from sudden death caused by accidents, suicide, homicide and other external causes (Burrell, Mehlum & Qin, 2018). It is commonly accepted that *sudden*, or *unanticipated death*, creates more difficulty for children's adjustment over time than does an anticipated death (Dunning, 2006). Sudden death has long been seen as more difficult to grieve than deaths for which there is prior warning (Worden, 1996). When a child's parent dies unexpectedly and there is no opportunity to prepare the child for the death, later adjustment can be problematic (Raveis, Siegel, & Karus, 1999) because a sudden death contributes to a tendency toward denial among survivors, which further leads to problematic adjustment in parentally bereaved children (Webb, 2010).

Although unanticipated death is commonly accepted as more difficult to children's adjustment than *anticipated* death, the opposite has been documented in a longitudinal study of the effects of parent death on children. This study found that the death of a parent following an illness lasting two or more weeks is linked to significantly more distress in children than those whose parent died suddenly. Moreover, lengthier illness correlated with worse outcomes for children after the parent's death (Kalter et al., 2002).

Saldinger et al. (1999) found that the lengthiest anticipations of the death of a parent were associated with the poorest adjustment for children post parental death. Researchers hypothesized that this may be because the anticipation of death or the stress of awaiting an approaching death may be more emotionally difficult on a child. The terminal illness of a parent presents the family with an experience outside the expected norm for the developmental stage of the child and the family. An anticipated death produces significant stress for adults and children, especially when the dying is prolonged (Dunning, 2006).

Factors surrounding anticipated death such as the length of illness, prior knowledge of the imminent death, or the degree to which the child is aware that the parent will die might affect the child's adjustment after the parent has died. The stresses of a fatal illness including alterations in lifestyle, the absence or withdrawal of the ill parent from family functions, and household economic changes are factors that might negatively affect a child pre-death and can continue to negatively affect the child until after the parent has died (Raveis, Siegel, & Karus, 1999).

In the following sections, we will explore how some of the different causes of death affect the way children respond to the loss of a parent.

Parental Suicide

Researchers have long debated whether suicide bereavement is different from anticipated and unanticipated grief (Webb, 2010). Melhem et al. (2007) concluded that complicated grief scores of children bereaved by suicide were similar to complicated grief scores of children bereaved by accidental or sudden natural deaths; however, it is possible that the unexpected nature of suicidal, accidental, and sudden natural deaths may have led to the similarity in complicated grief scores.

The central issue that complicates childhood bereavement resulting from unanticipated death, "is the formation of children's traumatic expectations about the world and a sense of worry about personal integrity and the security of interpersonal relationships" (Pfeffer, Karus, Siegel & Jiang, 2000, p. 2). These responses are associated with chronic symptoms of depression. Chronic depressive and behavioural symptoms are more prevalent in children whose parent died as a result of suicide than children whose parent died as a result of anticipated causes (Pfeffer et al., 200).

Many researchers conversely suggest that suicide bereavement differs in many ways from other types of grief in terms of the bereaved children's increased risk for psychopathology or poor social functioning as well as the potential stigma, shame, and isolation associated with suicide bereavement (Cain & Fast, 1966; Hung & Rabin, 2009; Pfeffer, 1981; Rutter, 1966; Shepherd & Barraclough, 1976). Furthermore, studies suggest that children are at a higher risk of attempting suicide if their parent died of suicide (Burrell et al., 2018). Specifically, girls who have lost a parent to suicide, are more likely than boys to attempt or complete suicide (Burrell et al., 2018).

Additionally, finding meaning from a suicidal death is more challenging for children than finding meaning following deaths from other causes (Webb, 2010). Jordan (2001) argues that some common survivor questions such as, "Why did they do it?", "Why didn't I prevent it?", and "How could they do this to me?" differentiates suicide bereavement and "may distinguish it from other losses, regardless of the measured intensity of the grief or psychiatric symptoms" (p. 92). Furthermore, suicide bereavement is a form of ***disenfranchised grief***, a term created by Doka (1989) and used to refer to a type of grief that individuals, including children, experience when a death cannot be "openly acknowledged, publicly mourned, or socially supported" (as cited in Webb, 2010, p. 111). Mourning children bereaved by suicide often feel stigmatized and may be looked upon more negatively by their peers and social group (Jordan, 2001). Children bereaved by suicide may be more emotionally dysfunctional, ashamed, depressed, self-blaming, and in need of psychological counseling (Jordan, 2001).

Death Caused by Terminal Illness

Children who lose a parent due to terminal illness such as cancer, have "exhibited symptoms of depression and associated psychological problems involving anxiety, behavioural problems, decreased social competence, and lower self-esteem" (Pfeffer et al., 2000, p. 1). Furthermore, Howell et al. (2016) put forth that losing a parent due to prolonged disease increases the risk of "maladaptive grief and posttraumatic stress symptoms" (p. 153) compared to losing a parent to sudden death. Research claims that prolonged hospital visits, parental unavailability, and the notion of separation is a struggle for children to experience. However, studies have also found that when a parent with a terminal illness communicates their illness to their child and what is to come (death), the child displays a better psychosocial adjustment after the loss (Howell et al., 2016). It is important for children to know what to expect rather than leaving them in question and confusion because this will complicate their grief process (Howell et al., 2016).

Death Caused by Natural Disasters

Losing a parent during a natural disaster, has been associated with the occurrence of post-traumatic stress disorder symptoms (Haine, Ayers, Sandler & Wolchik, 2008). A study conducted by Kalantari and Vostanis (2010) found that children who had lost a parent during an earthquake displayed high levels of behavioural and emotional problems. Furthermore, educators that worked with children who had lost a parent during a natural disaster reported that children exhibited more emotional and peer relationship problems, while the remaining parent of the child reported more behavioural problems. After natural disasters, the surviving family members, including children, need many services to support them through their challenge. Kalantari and Vostanis (2010) claim that "parents and teachers should receive training/mental health promotion aimed at learning how to help the surviving children cope with their loss; improving the recognition of continuing child mental health problems; and managing such problems at home and at school" (p. 166). These services should be long-term to ensure that the families and their children have readjusted to their new life (Kalantari & Vostanis, 2010).

Death Caused by Crime

Children who experience violent forms of parental death display "symptoms of depression, severe anxiety, hyperarousal, and intrusive thoughts within the first year after parental death" (Pfeffer et al., 2000, p. 1). What is even more challenging for children is experiencing a **parental intimate partner homicide**. Every year, over 55, 000 children worldwide are bereaved by intimate partner homicide, where one parent is the victim (deceased) and one parent is the offender (detained). These children lose their home, and sometimes their school and friends. Research indicates that such children display strong grief reactions, developmental difficulties and posttraumatic stress disorders (Alisic, et al., 2015). Furthermore, clinicians claim that many of these children "become 'high-end' users of mental health and social services over multiple years, even decades" (Alisic, et al., 2015, p. 1).

IMPACT OF REMAINING PARENT'S RESPONSE

Factors that may influence the adjustment of parentally bereaved children include both child-level and family-level variables. Several family-level variables, such as the adjustment of the remaining parent and the quality of care received by the child after the loss, are significantly related to how children cope (Kalter et al., 2002). When a parent dies, life changes for the child, the remaining parent, and the family because a vital member is missing (Worden, 1996). The impact of loss for the remaining family members is often colossal (Rothaupt & Becker, 2007).

The loss of a significant person, along with the roles played by that person, can throw the family system off balance (Worden, 1996). When faced with the stress and anxiety that develops from the death of a parent, families commonly become emotionally overwhelmed and reactive to each other (Rothaupt & Becker, 2007).

The child's adjustment to the death is influenced by the way in which the family, and especially the remaining parent, responds to this loss (Kalter et al., 2002). How the remaining parent copes with the loss of their partner affects how their children work through the tasks of grief (Kirwin & Hamrin, 2005). With the death of a spouse, the remaining parent is forced into the new role of a single parent, he or she must deal with his or her own reactions to the death, and the remaining parent must respond to his or her child's needs (Worden, 1996). The remaining parent may not be prepared for managing his or her own reactions as well as the reactions of the child (Howarth, 2011); however, the degree to which a parent can meet both sets of needs will affect how well the child responds and adjusts to the loss and the changes in his or her life (Worden, 1996).

According to Worden (1996), bereaved children need three things to help them cope with the disruption in the family system caused by the death of a parent: support, nurturance, and continuity. The child will feel supported when the remaining parent can function as a teacher and guide, providing feedback, and encouragement about the child's feelings and behaviour following the death. A nurturing parent provides food, clothing, and shelter, but most importantly, he or she listens to the child and uses this information to help the child. Continuity is frequently overlooked when considering children's needs after the death of a parent; however, the child's world has changed forever and each bereaved child needs a sense that the family will continue, with connection between the past and the future (Worden, 1996). Frequently, however, the remaining parent does not recognize a child's grief responses and needs. Sometimes, remaining parents may be too absorbed by their own grief; therefore, they become unavailable and experience difficulties in supporting the child, talking about death, sharing feelings, and answering the child's questions (Papadatou et al., 2002). Raveis, V., Siegel, K., & Karus, M. (1999) explain, "a recent analysis of data from the Memorial Sloan-Kettering bereavement study found that the child's perception of the surviving parent's level of openness in general communication was highly correlated with the child's level of distress" (as cited in Christ, 2000, p. 20).

After the death of a spouse, the remaining parent not only needs to process his or her grief, but he or she also has to adjust the way he or she has parented in response to the absence of his or her co-parent. This adjustment may happen progressively, in cases of long illnesses or may be sudden, in the case of a traumatic sudden death. Remaining parents transition from dual parenting roles to single parenting; therefore, the remaining parent will need to find a way to take on the role of both parents (Glazer, Clark, Thomas, & Haxton, 2010). Nickman, Silverman, and Normand (1998) present three basic suggestions for remaining parents to support their grieving children. First, the remaining parent should acknowledge the child's loss and his or her feelings as a result of the loss. Second, that the remaining parent considers the child when making decisions related to the deceased, such as disposal of possessions, recognizing that these now concern the whole family. Third, the remaining parent should be cautious about making changes in the family structure without talking to the child first. Following these guidelines conveys to children that their feelings are being respected, and that the family process that existed when the deceased parent was alive is being sustained.

There are two factors that can significantly impact the ways in which remaining parents contribute to their children's response to parental death. First, if the remaining parent experienced death of a family member in childhood, the remaining parent might model their own parent's reactions to their needs at the time. Porterfield, Cain & Saldinger (2003) executed a series of interviews with 41 bereaved spouses and their children. They stated, "a full 79% of study participants recalled at least one example of a way in which their loss experience as a child influenced subsequent parenting of their grieving children" (Porterfield, Cain & Saldinger, 2003, p.205). The remaining parent's experiences with death will directly affect the way that they fulfill their children's needs in the moment of the loss of their parent. However, Porterfield, Cain & Salinger (2003) clearly point out that the connection does not follow a discernable pattern since the reaction differs from person to person, based on factors such as their experience and their personality.

Second, another factor that may influence the remaining parent's contribution to children's grief is whether or not the remaining parent has utilized therapy to further understand their own grief and their child's. Werner-Lin & Biank (2013) explain, "bereaved spouses must engage with their own grief so that they can attend to their child's grief-related and developmental needs" (p. 2). Their subsequent study on a therapy program demonstrated that parents need to understand the ways that children grieve and how to recognize that grief. The program used open communication and slow implementation of change to routines to help the remaining parent work through their own grief. "This portion of the program reduced the burden on surviving parents as well as on parentified children, and increased feelings of safety by opening family dialogue about fears" (Werner-Lin & Biank, 2013, p. 11).

Childhood Loss and Grief

CASE STUDIES

Erica

My name is Erica. When I was 8 years old, my father died from ALS, Lou Gehrig's disease. I am 25 now. When my father became sick, I pretended to be stronger than I was. I was shy to talk about it. In fact, I hardly ever wanted to talk about it. I had prepared myself for his death and became aware that he was going to pass away, so when it happened, I didn't cry. Although I knew my father was sick, I was not aware of the timeline they had given his life. I was not aware that it would have come to an end so quickly, and for this, I am often thankful.

I was so young when my father died, but losing him pushed me to mature in myself and appreciate the time I am able to spend with the people in my life. I remember the illness and the way it changed our lives, the way my father and I were able to interact. I remember my father taking me to the park, somewhere he could sit while I played. I remember other parents pushing their children on the swings. I was able to spend a lot of time with him, as I was in school for half days, and I would take care of him—especially since he was in a wheelchair. These were the days that my appreciation and understanding, for my father and his illness, grew stronger and deeper.

I tried to take on a lot as a child after my father passed. I wanted to be there as much as I could for my mom. I matured very fast. I never stopped working [I started when I was thirteen]. I maintained my commitment to sports teams. I tried to keep myself as busy as I could. I felt like when I wasn't doing anything, I would be thinking about it.

My father's death affected me in psychological and emotional ways. I knew that he was different from other parents and that he was in a wheelchair. I knew that what he could now do, physically, was different. Although, I understood [in the best way that I could] these changes, the children around me did not. They would always tell me that they were sorry, but they couldn't fully understand what they were sorry for. On Father's Day and around his birthday, I would feel the pain and the void a little more. I felt like sort of an outsider during these periods.

I tried to maintain a normal and active type of participation in my school work. My mother was a teacher and instilled this in me; that I would always have to try, although she never pressured me. I think that this helped me choose my path in life. Now I want to help children, and be a positive influence in their lives. I want to be like the teacher that I once had, who made me feel better and like I could overcome anything. The kind of teacher that takes the time to know you and understand you. I feel that when it came to choosing my life path, this experience and the teacher I had were huge influences.

My brothers took my father's passing differently. My brothers were teenagers when he passed, they tried to avoid the feelings and, I guess I could say they acted out. One of my brothers got kicked out of school, a few times. While the other just kept himself super busy, working two jobs and maintaining school work.

My mom, well, she mostly kept how she felt to herself after losing my father, her husband. She was very upset, maybe even depressed and she didn't talk about it a lot. She kept herself busy through work, she was a teacher, and she maintained her prior hobbies; yoga, art, she was into a lot. She would travel with us a lot, I think that may even be how she coped: *don't talk about it, just bring them to places and do things with them so they are happy*. I think it was just something she needed to learn how to cope with as well, on her own, without needing to talk about it all the time. She was sad for quite some time. I thought it was really great to watch her *move on*, and be happy again. My brothers had a harder time with it than me, but I really love my stepdad. He and my mother share a different love than the one she shared with my dad – it's amazing.

We had a lot of support from the neighbourhood. They were generous with their time and their efforts to help us through the time. Some would offer to mow our lawn and shovel our driveway. They would also bring us food; they just really wanted to show their support for us.

My relationship with my brothers and my mother definitely changed after my father passed away. I am very close with one of my brothers, the one that decided to stay busy after my father passed. My other brother, it took us a while to become close. When he was a teenager he would run away, and just did some things that I couldn't agree with. Today we are very close, but it has taken years for us all to get to this point.

Today, I have a two [and a half] year old daughter and am engaged to be married. I was very particular with the person I chose to be the father of my child; I wanted someone who was going to be an involved father and be a role model in their lives. I wanted someone who was going to do activities with her, and share the load of parenthood. I know how important it is to have a great father figure, like mine was.

My brothers have yet to settle down. I think losing our dad affected them more, they were older and lost out on having a father figure to guide them through their critical years. I think they fear becoming fathers, in a way.

I still talk to my dad around the date. We listen to his music; he was a musician. Around Christmas we will play his songs, he named a lot of them after us. That's how we keep his memory alive, through his music. We show my daughter all of his music, although she will never meet him, we involve him in her life through his songs.

Overall, losing my father was a horrible experience, but something that I had to live through. It has affected the person I was, the relationships I have with my family, and the person I am today. It is sad to not have him, and it was sad to lose him, but even though he is gone, his impact and who he was will never be forgotten. It has made me who I am today. He will always be with us, through his music and our memories, and those are what I cherish today.

Vanessa

My name is Vanessa. I am currently 25 years old. When I was 10 years old, my father died of cancer. Being 10 years old, I was aware that my father was ill. I remember visiting my father regularly in the hospital and creating "welcome home" signs due to my excitement for when he was able to come home. However, looking back, I believe that I convinced myself that sickness eventually passes. The thought of my father dying and leaving my siblings and I without a father, and my mother without a husband, never crossed my mind.

Being as I was so young when my father died, I feel as though I blocked many childhood memories out of my mind, especially those surrounding my father's illness. I mostly remember being sad and confused regarding my father's illness because I felt as though my family was falling apart and due to my age, I felt like my family wanted to protect me from knowing the worst that was yet to come.

I remember finding out that my father had cancer at my grandmother's house with the rest of my family, including my father's sisters and brother. I cannot recall anyone specifically telling me the seriousness of my father's illness, but I understood the circumstances of the situation by observating everyone's reaction. All I can remember is that I was told that my father was sick with cancer, but my family barely spoke about his illness around me. I remember being confused and sad when I found out my father was sick. I did not understand what life was going to be like. 25 years later, no one could have prepared me for the way my life changed and continues to change due to the absence of a father figure.

Although I don't remember my childhood as vividly as most individuals would, the day my father died is a day I will never forget. Every morning, I would kiss my mom and dad goodbye before going to school, but that morning, my dad was overly tired and he was sleeping. I didn't kiss him goodbye. Shortly after arriving to school, I got called down to the office and my mom's sister was there to pick me up. While crying, she told me that my dad was not doing well and she was bringing me to the hospital to see him.

As we arrived at the hospital, I remember feeling a different energy amongst my family. Everyone was sad, quiet, and crying. I knew this was not like any normal visit with my dad at the hospital. My dad was in the emergency room and a number of hours passed, I was told that I had to say my final goodbyes to my father. There I stood, in the room with my mom and two sisters, in denial that this was the last time I was ever going to see or speak to my dad.

Following my father's passing, I remember being sad, angry, and in denial. I do not remember how I coped with the death of my father. It is all sort of a blur to me. I do not think I ever came to terms with his death, which is why I believe that I blocked out so many childhood memories I had with my father: the good and the bad.

After my father died, my life changed in many ways. Not only were my two sisters and I left without a father, but my mother was left without a husband and a support system. The dynamics of the family changed. We grew apart from my dad's side of the family and I learned many things about my family that my father withheld from us. I felt like my whole world was collapsing. My only support system was my mother, my sisters, and my mother's side of the family, including her best friend and her sister. Although I did have a support system, we were all dealing with our own losses in our own ways. Being the youngest, I also felt like my family did not want to discuss the events that occurred following my dad's death, in order to protect me. This caused me to withdraw from telling my family about my feelings as I felt like a bother to my sisters and my mother who were also dealing with the loss of my dad.

Growing up without a father, some days are "easier" than others, but it is never easy. At 25 years old, there is always a memory of what was and what could have been if things had been different, which is the root of the anxiety that I continue to suffer with today. Reflecting back, I was not aware of how much my life would change. Now as an adult, one of my biggest fears is change. After my father died, I moved houses and because my family dynamics changed, I feared that my school and friend life would also change. I believed that I would be known as the "girl whose dad died" and I believed that my emotions would not allow me to build relationships with others. I was scared of getting attached to individuals, in fear of losing them, just as I lost my dad.

I was always a homebody, but I began to understand the importance of family and wanting to spend time with the people I loved most, which encouraged me to spend as much time with my mom and sisters as I could. I realized that we never have enough time with the people we love.

Growing up, I also had anxiety about money. My father and his family had a large beauty company which was where the majority of our family income came from. When my father passed, I feared that my mother would not be able to take care of us because she was a stay at home mom. Being so young, I was unaware of the circumstances of money or my father's will. This anxiety followed me into adulthood as I am now precautious with money. Moreover, I am precautious with every decision I make. It takes me a long time to make decisions, even for little things like whether or not I should have a peanut butter sandwich with jelly or without jelly. I fear that every decision I make will change the course of my life.

As silly as it seems to some people, I understand that my anxiety roots from my childhood. I have gone to counseling to discuss my childhood as well as the feelings it has surfaced for me in my adult life. I have come to understand that my past is something that will always be with me and will continue to impact many events that occur in my life.

Considering this, my mom is one of the most important people in my life. Following my father's passing, the dynamics of my family changed. My mother took on the role of my mother and my father and she had to raise three children on her own. My sisters and I were forced to grow up and mature faster than other children our age. Because of this, I have created a special bond with my mom and my sisters that I am grateful for. We have been through so much together, more than other individuals can recognize and they have become my best friends and biggest supporters throughout my whole life.

Although my father is gone, he is never forgotten. My family and I keep my father's presence alive in so many ways. We reminisce about our memories together, watch his favorite movies, listen to his favorite songs, and we always look for symbols that he sends us from heaven. We make sure that although he is physically gone, he is never forgotten and his presence is always with us. Because of this, I do not fear my mother moving on because my father is someone we can never move on from or forget. Instead, I hope that in our lifetime, we can find peace and happiness when it comes to our past.

I understand that my past is something that I cannot change. I can only hope and wish that things were different and I still had my dad by my side. But, in all my triumphs and tribulations, I know that he is always by my side, watching over me and guiding me throughout my adulthood. I will not be able to have a father-daughter dance, nor will my sisters' children or my own children ever meet their grandfather. But, one thing I know is that my dad's presence and character lives on through the bond my sisters and I made with my mom, a bond that I am grateful for.

Mike

I have two children, Lauren and Sarah; they were three and five when my wife Sandra passed away. Today, my daughters are five and seven. My wife, Sandra, committed suicide by hanging herself. It was tough to understand; why she would do this and how to explain this to my children, I had no idea where to start.

I believed my children were too young to understand the concept of suicide; it took me almost three months to explain the aspects of it. I then decided to take my children to a family therapist. I had read many articles that said it was better to tell your children about things like this early on; when they develop their identity, something like this should be a part of them, not something that shatters them later on in life. Three months later, I took them to where Sandra, their mother, hung herself. We talked and I tried to explain why something like this would have happened; we talked about mental illness and how it can make someone, like their mom, believe that this was their only option. They both had a hard time understanding, my youngest especially.

My girls started to worry that something was going to happen to them, to me. My eldest, Lauren, she worried that she had the same disease as her mom. I had to explain that most people don't do what their mother did, even if they may have a same type of mental illness. People with mental illness, they get help other ways; people take medicine, they go to therapy, they don't all commit suicide.

My girls dealt with their grief in ways that only a child can see fit. They would be sad one moment, and the next they would want to go outside to play. Their therapist had mentioned that this would happen. That their grief may seem like it is gone, but at different periods of their life it may come back. I can see this within myself as well; when I think that I am past it, I am reminded of my grief on birthdays and anniversaries, through different periods.

Today, my girls still face the same struggles, but have learned ways to cope. Sarah, my youngest, she has become aggressive with her sister and with myself. I think often times she is acting this way to express how she feels inside; she is putting everything together and expressing her emotions in ways she couldn't before. Lauren, my eldest, she just keeps going. Often times I can sense that they are sad but we talk about Sandra every day. We kept memories of her around the house and find ourselves saying little things like, *"Mommy wouldn't like this."*

Chapter Four: The Death of a Parent

When Sandra passed, Lauren was in kindergarten and Sara was in day care and I was a stay at home dad. Being a stay at home dad; being the person who dropped them off and picked them up from school, made them lunch, and watched them while Sandra worked, made the transition of only having me around, *easier*.

Lauren tries to take on the role of a protector in the family, a maternal role. I was always making the point that they need to be kids right now, nothing else. But, I think it comes naturally for her as an older sister, she feels the need to play this role. Sara, I think she is still very young to have been affected in her role as a child. It is my job to be the parent and protect my children, this is what I try and keep at the forefront of their development through role change.

Lauren's school and Sara's daycare were very supportive after Sandra passed. The teachers are very mindful of the girls and pay close attention to their good and bad days. The girl's friends are also very supportive of them. We started seeing a therapist when Sandra was concerned that her depression was affecting the girls; we would see the therapist just us two [Sandra and I] and as a family. I was grateful that we had already had this person in our lives, it made it easier when trying to find new support. My girls took part in an eight-week bereavement program which allowed them to connect with other children in similar situations. The program focused on helping children talk about their feelings although our experience did not lack communication; we were always very open and I wanted to make sure they knew that I would answer any of their questions. It [suicide] is nothing to be ashamed of, I was always open to talking and answering any questions the girls may have had. My father died in 9/11; I am not a stranger to unexpected and traumatic loss, although it may hurt, there are ways to heal and talking about it was always very important to me. I remember my therapist telling me that the way a person dies is not who the person was. I try to relay this to my children as often as I can. The way Sandra died does not explain her whole life, there were many wonderful things about her.

I made time to grieve on my own and with the girls. When I start to cry or get sad while the girls are around, I do not remove myself from the situation but instead we talk about it. We don't share everything and I don't think it is important for me to tell them every part of the grief I face, but we are definitely open. I want to make sure they know that it is ok to cry, to feel sad and to show their emotion. My youngest, Sara, takes out her emotion through anger. I ensure that she knows it is ok to feel angry; angry at her mom for doing what she did, angry at me and angry at the way things are now. Lauren, my oldest, fears after life. She fears that this is the only life she gets to live and that nothing will happen next. I tell her that no one knows what comes next but that it is important to make the most of our time here. These are the worries and emotions of my young children. It is important to know their fears and their feelings, it is important that we work on these together.

As time passes, I fear that my children will suffer from depression the way their mother did. I fear that one or both of them will end their lives the way Sandra did. I don't know if I will ever feel safe or secure knowing that they might do exactly what she did, at any point in their lives. I also fear, as they get older they will become angry with the situation and that they will rebel.

I think my girls are pretty secure with our relationship. There is a woman in my life, and I feel that the girls will benefit from having a female role in their lives. They have always gravitated toward the female energy because they don't have that in their life right now. It will be a transition period for sure but they are aware that some aspects of our lives with have to change. I will have to go to work, meaning someone else will replace the home care role that I used to have. For me, I feel like moving on means that I am saying goodbye to Sandra, but I know that I will always keep her memory alive, for myself and for my girls.

The girls do artwork and bake to keep their mother's memory alive. Sandra used to love to paint and bake. We try to keep our schedule the same and travel if we can; we used to travel every summer and camp out. Sara always likes to look through old photos and videos and listen to stories about Sandra. I always encourage Sandra's family to tell them stories about when she was little girl. I am still very close with Sandra's family. Sandra's sister has been my closest support through this time. I feel that they will always be my family, we have become closer than ever.

If I were to share any advice for families going through this, it would mainly be to just talk to their kids. The importance of communication and openness. Treat your children as equals and not as fragile beings who need to protected from the truth. To use this traumatic experience as something that brings your family together and makes your bond stronger. To not be ashamed of the circumstances under which you lost a loved one, but to be a provider of answers to questions from anyone who is asking. To not go into isolation and grieve on your own.

I wish that my wife was still here; I wish that I could have done or said something different. But these are the circumstances that I cannot change. Every day we continue to move forward, as a unit. I will continue to support my children and be the best father that I can be; checking up on my girls and making sure they know they always have me to talk to, cry with, and smile with. It has been a challenging time to say the least, but it will and it does get better.

Mary

When my husband, my children's father died, they were 16, 13, and 10 years old. Three amazing girls headed to young adulthood.

Fourteen years have gone by in a blink of an eye. My daughters are 30, 27, and 24 now. The two oldest are married with children of their own.

When telling your story, it's always best to start at the beginning. My husband was diagnosed on March 24, 2003 with non-Hodgkin's Lymphoma. He passed away on March 25, 2004. One year plus one day after diagnosis.

At the time, my husband and I were separated. But there was no hesitation on my part to help him through this journey. I never wanted my kids to look at me and think, "You didn't help our dad." So, my kids were already in a state of disbelief, panic, and sadness that their parents were not together. Then cancer was added to the mix.

It was a very hard year for my children and myself. Unfortunately, he was diagnosed during the SARS outbreak, so it was difficult and sometimes impossible to see him while he was having treatment. The cancer had paralyzed him, so he was in a rehab centre. I would video tape my kids to show my husband and video tape him to show my kids.

It was very hard on my kids. They essentially lost both parents. We had to rely on my family and my best friend to help out.

Because I truly believed that my husband would beat it, I think my children thought the same. Towards the end, it was obvious to anyone, including my children, this was a fight he would not win.

Throughout the year, there were good days, bad days, long days, lonely days. I tried my best to balance taking care of everyone, but I know that to some degree, I failed my kids. I was hell bent on saving their father that I fell short on taking care of their needs.

I never asked my kids if they had conversations with their dad. I didn't want to intrude. I kept stressing to him that he needed to somehow impact their lives. Only they know if he did or not.

After he passed, we were broken. So, deep in my sadness and guilt of not being able to save him that it affected how my children grieved. I was angry that this had happened to us and it made my children angry.

I know that my kids were afraid of my moving on, but what they didn't know or understand at the time is that I made a promise to their dad that they would be my priority. They would want for nothing, they would do well in school, be accomplished all in their own way, and I would be secondary.

I could see changes in them. My oldest took on the role as the caregiver and advisor and always tried to be more mature than she needed to be—still to this day. My middle child's sadness was heighted by her anger at the world and her anger at me. To the point that she had convinced herself that I didn't care or love her. We became estranged for over a year. My baby became angry, lashing out, especially at school. She was anxious and had a hard time making decisions. She still does. She was frightened about our financial situation even though I reassured her that we were fine.

What united us as a force to be reckoned with and still keeps us tethered to each other is that my husband's family turned their backs on us. That, and him dying, has made us four strong, smart, ambitious, courageous, empathetic, sympathetic, amazing women. All of my kids are perusing and achieving their goals.

What was once a force of four has become a family of ten and we are not finished yet. We are closer than ever and no one and nothing will get between us.

We talk about him, remember him, good and bad. We tell the grandkids about him and we speak to him and know that he is there with us.

After all of these years, I still have fears and worries. I fear that I wasn't enough. That my kids will always look back thinking, "Dad should have been there." I fear that when I am gone, my kids will drift apart. I worry that my kids will have to take care of me. I don't want to be a burden on them.

Nadia

Time…it's a funny thing. We don't see it or feel it passing us by, but there it goes, carrying with it our most precious memories and moments. I fear time, mostly because I worry I won't remember the things I've left behind but also because I'm anxious for what the future holds. I guess everyone feels the same way. Life and time is the same for everyone, but not all our stories are the same.

I often sit back and think about my childhood and teenage years. When I think about my childhood, I feel love, I feel happiness, I hear laughter and see joy. I grew up in your typical Italian family. I had my wonderful mother and father and my two amazing sisters. I have an older sister by three years and a younger sister by three years. Our age gap never got in the way of our relationship and time spent together. Me and my sisters loved to play and have fun together. Our days were filled with nothing but playing and having fun. Having sisters was one of the best parts about being a kid because we did everything together and I was so grateful to have them.

Our parents loved us tremendously. Our father worked hard to make sure we had everything we needed and our mother was a stay at home who took care of all of our needs. Our parents always made sure we were happy and felt loved and we always had a close relationship with them. Me and my sisters were actually known as the kids who had the "cool" parents. Everyone loved coming to our house and being with our mom and playing with our toys.

So many people I knew were divorced or getting divorced, some within our family. And while all these other marriages were falling apart my parents were so in love. I can still see them dancing together, laughing and joking around, driving in the car and holding hands the entire time, and hugging and kissing one another. My parents showed me and my sisters the beauty in love not only in the way they loved us but in the way that they loved each other. I thought we had the picture-perfect family and life, but life was aiming to throw me a curve ball that I was never expecting and it hit me dead on when I was thirteen years old.

The first sign that something was wrong was when my dad got back from a business trip and took me and my sisters out to a movie. Not even half way through the movie I remember my dad getting up and not being able to sit back down and complaining that it was his back. He left the theatre and went to the bathroom several times but it only seemed to be getting worse. On our way home we needed to pull over so that my dad could get out and have a break from sitting. I can still feel the worry I had that day looking at my dad in pain and not really understanding what was happening and why. Me and my sisters went home and told my mom what happened and I remember her telling us not to worry that she was sure everything was fine.

A couple of weeks later we went to Dave and Busters with our dad. That day was the beginning of what would turn out to be the worst year. He was in a lot of pain that day, not really acting like himself and struggling to keep up with us. Me and my sisters were doing a car race when my dad said that he was going to the bathroom and would be back. A long time passes and my dad was nowhere to be seen. We walked around looking for him but we couldn't find him. It seemed impossible that he could have been in the bathroom for that long, so my older sister approached a security guard and asked him to go check the bathroom for our dad. After a few minutes the security guard came out and told us our dad was in there and would be out soon. I can still picture my dad's face when he did come out of that bathroom, he was pale white, sweaty, and shaky. He looked at us and half smiled. I can still remember the feeling in my heart. We got home and again told our mom what happened and this time the worry was written all over her face too. What followed was a bunch of doctor's appointments and tests to figure out just what was causing my dad all his pain. The results were something we could have never imagined.

One of the most vivid memories I have is the night I found out my dad was sick. It was March 24, 2003. My mom and my grandfather brought my dad to the doctor while me and my sisters waited with my aunts and grandmother at her house. I was in the living room with my sisters when the door opened and my parents walked inside. I can still see my grandmother walking to meet them at the door, I can see her embracing my dad and I can hear the cries coming from everyone and in that moment, my breath was taken away. I froze, I didn't finish my walk to the door and I didn't have to because as I stopped walking my mom started on her way toward me with the look of complete devastation.

She told me and my sisters that there was something she needed to tell us and for us to sit down. She told us that the reason my dad hadn't been feeling well was because he was sick. He had cancer; lymphoma to be exact. I knew what cancer was, a few people in our family had already suffered with this illness. I knew it was bad but I didn't really understand the severity of the kind my dad had. All I could think to myself was how and why? Why my dad? Why my family? We all cried but my mom told us everything was going to be okay and not to worry.

When I walked out of the room my dad was standing there. I can still picture his face now and what it looked like as I looked up at him through tear-filled eyes. He didn't have one tear. He was smiling at me and hugged me. I sobbed and he whispered in my ear, "Don't cry. I'm going to be okay." Oh, how much my 13-year-old self wished that was true. I held onto those words just as tightly as I held on to my dad, but sometimes no matter how tightly you hold onto something, it will find a way to slip away.

We only had one short year and a day with my dad after that diagnosis, but while it wasn't enough time, it seemed to go on forever. I have to be honest; some of my memories from that year are a blur. From what I remember, too much time passed before my dad was diagnosed and all the while his tumor grew stronger and bigger. The tumor was so big that it pushed up against his spine and he was paralyzed.

Seeing him in that wheelchair was so hard for me. Here was this man that was larger than life. He was always dancing and having fun, and he was no longer even able to walk. Because of my dad's condition he was admitted into a rehabilitation centre which was difficult on its own, but what made it worse was me and my sisters were not able to see him for a long time in the beginning because there was a SARS outbreak and children were not permitted in the hospital. My mom tried her best to make the most of this situation by having us send him videos and him sending them back, but it just wasn't the same.

Finally, the day came that we were approved to go see my dad. I remember being so happy and so scared all at the same time. I wanted to see my dad but I wanted the dad from all my beautiful memories, not the dad who was stuck in a chair, thin and frail, bald, and so sick. But my dad was different and not just because he was sick, but because this illness was taking his self-esteem and happiness.

When my dad was finally approved for weekend visits at home, we bought him a wheelchair accessible van. I have never talked about this before to anyone, it is one of my memories I think about all the time and it still hurts me to this day. The first weekend we brought my dad home, I rode in the van with him and my grandfather. I got into the van first and sat in the back seat and then a nurse helped my dad lock himself in place. When he shut the door, my dad put his head down and cried. For a moment, I didn't react, but then I leaned forward put my hand on him and asked if he was okay. All he could manage was a nod. I sat back and silently cried. I was mad, I was sad and I wanted to be strong for him in that moment but I didn't know how. I wished all of this would just go away but it was just the beginning.

Things eventually settled down enough that my dad was able to come home permanently. I believed in my heart that he was going to beat this and him not having to stay at the hospital anymore was the first sign to me that he was. For the first time in a long time, I felt happy. We were all going to be together again because not only was I getting my dad back, but I would get my mom back, too.

When my dad was in the hospital my mom spent a lot of time away from home. While I understood my dad needed her and she needed to be with him, I missed her so much. My mom was always with me and my sisters, we did everything together and she was an amazing mom. Then my dad got sick and she was gone. I did feel in a way I was losing both my parents and I couldn't wait to have them back.

Cancer came home with my parents and it was ugly. It brought with it horrible days and memories. We spent so much more time crying than laughing in those days and the more time that passed, the more angry I became. I was confused because each time I thought my dad was getting worse something would happen that gave me a sense of hope. He eventually was able to walk again with his walker. I thought he was going to be okay and that he was beating it. But he wasn't. It was just a small ray of light in our dark days. This only confused me more because I was having so many emotions all at once and I couldn't wrap my head around it because I didn't really understand it.

I believe a lot of my anger and confusion was because I was at an awkward stage in my life when all of this was happening. I was stuck between feeling like I should be told everything that was going on because I deserved to know and could handle it and feeling so small and scared. I would get information through listening to conversations but I think my own hopes tainted a lot of what I knew was happening. If I heard things about him not doing well, I would shut down and ignore it. When I heard people talking about his good days, I would reassure myself that I was right about him beating this. I had so much going on inside my head but I never really liked to talk about it and I never wanted to ask questions. I was scared to ask something and know the complete truth and not being able to lie to myself anymore.

Chapter Four: The Death of a Parent

I worried about upsetting people by asking the wrong thing or saying the wrong thing when everyone was already so upset. There was no hiding from what was going on at home, it was everywhere I turned. At school, I was able to pretend that everything was okay even if they knew I was lying. If someone at school asked about my dad or how I was doing I would just say we were both good and change the subject. I had so many people at school who wanted to be there for me and I just pushed them to the side. I thought by lying about what was happening it would somehow go away and figured that they could never understand anyway. The truth is I really never even gave anyone the chance to understand me. I could never find the words to express myself about how I felt and what was going on, so I just didn't say anything at all. In that year, I lied to myself a lot. I lied to myself about my dad being okay, about my mom being okay, about my sisters being okay and most of all about myself being okay. I wanted it to be true but it was far from true. The truth is it would be a long time before we could say we were okay.

My dad's illness affected the relationships that I had with other's in my life. I always looked up to my mom. I always had a great relationship with my mom. She was easy to talk to and always made sure we were talking about everything. She was fun and funny and I loved spending time with her. She brought me so much comfort and confidence as a child. I always knew I was lucky to have her, but I would be lying if I said that year didn't bring on a change. She had to care for her three young girls while caring for her very ill husband, and she never wavered in any of her duties. She made sure me and my sisters were still taken care of while making sure my dad was comfortable and okay; she made sure we were always on time for school and picked up at the end of the day, while still making sure my dad made it to every one of his doctor appointments; our fridge was always full; there was always dinner on the table and our clothes were always washed and anything we needed was fulfilled. But while she kept all our lives full, my mom was empty.

Her smiles grew fewer and far between and the ones she had were only on her face and not in her heart. I could see the pain in my mom's face every time I looked at her and I saw how much she was dealing with that I never wanted to bother her with my own feelings and questions. I didn't want to be an extra burden. I don't remember ever sitting with my mom and having an open discussion about my dad's illness, how I saw the change in her, and how I was changing.

As more and more time passed, I ached to have my mom back, just as much as I ached for my dad to get better. It was another confusing thing for me, because I understood and knew my mom was doing what she needed to do and that it was hard for her to do it all. But, I was sad and mad. I think about what I felt then and I'm embarrassed because I was so selfish. I felt like I was last and was being forgotten and what a horrible thing to focus on while there were so many more important things going on. I let these emotions take over and once I was engulfed in them, I couldn't find my way out. I felt more alone and misunderstood than ever before.

My relationship with my mom wasn't the only thing that changed. I lost parts of my sisters, too. The biggest loss was the relationship I had with my older sister. We were as close as could be before my dad got sick. We fought like all siblings do, but we were inseparable. But when my dad was sick, play time was over…literally. We enjoyed time together less because we didn't enjoy our time; we just went through it. We walked by each other in our own house like we were strangers. We hardly talked, and, for some reason, any conversation turned into a fight. My older sister became like another parent to me and my little sister. We were so awful to her for it though, because we fought against it. Instead of appreciating what she was doing for me and leaning on her because she was giving me the chance to, I was mad at her for thinking she could and should take care of me. I wanted her to just go back to being my sister and my parents being my parents. My sister was putting aside her own hurt to help me and my little sister through ours, but we threw it back in her face. How unfortunate that I never knew what I had at the time. I still have regrets over how I treated my sister. I appreciate and admire her strength so much now. I just wish I did then, too.

My relationship with my little sister wasn't affected in as big of a way because she was so small. I felt like I had to protect her, in some way, and the only way I knew how was to pretend that what was happening–wasn't. I think the biggest mistake I made with her was pushing her aside because she was so young. I assumed she didn't know or understand because she was so young, but I should have been there more for her. I realize now that age isn't a factor when it comes to suffering and death and that she should have never been dismissed. I still wish I sat with her and asked her how she was doing or feeling instead of just pretending everything was okay. I realize now that just like I needed someone to ask me how I was, so did my sisters and I missed the opportunity to ask them.

March 24, 2004 was the beginning of the end. It was a regular morning in the house. My older sister had already left for school; me and my little sister were getting ready for school. I can't recall what was happening at school that day but I do know I was rushing out of the house to go to school early. I was at the door waiting for my mom to come say goodbye. I could see into my dad's room which had moved to the main floor. He stirred in his sleep and then opened his eyes, he looked at me and smiled and then closed his eyes again. My decision to not go into his room and kiss him or talk to him when I saw him wake up has haunted me ever since. It will until my dying day, as that was the last time my dad ever looked at me and smiled.

I went to school and not long after the start of the day I was paged to go to the office. Walking down to the office I had a feeling in my gut that something just wasn't right, and it wasn't. I got to the office and the principal called me into her room. She sat me down and explained to me that my dad had to be rushed to the hospital and that my aunt was coming to pick me up to bring me there. I burst into tears.

I was inconsolable and the principal called my teacher down to talk to me. My teacher told me that I had to be strong and brave for my dad, but most of all for my little sister who they hadn't told yet. My teacher explained to me that they felt it was best that I be the one to tell her, because she was so young and would need me. I was petrified. How could they leave this task to me? I was so young. How could I possibly be the best choice for her?

When she walked in, she asked me what was going on, and I told her our aunt was coming to get us and she asked me if it was because of our dad. I told her yes and that he was in the hospital. She cried and hugged me. She asked me if he was going to die and I told her the honest truth; that I didn't know, but if he did he would want us there and that she had to try to be brave. We walked out of the room and my aunt stood there with swollen red eyes and I knew I was going to lose my dad that day.

When we got to the hospital, we walked into the emergency room. There stood my older sister behind my mom who was sitting in a chair holding my dad's hand and the only thing I could feel was fear. I pushed myself up against the wall and shut my eyes. I wanted it all to disappear and I didn't want to be there. My mom came up to me crying and told me to go to my dad. I told her no and she cried. She told me that my dad hadn't woke up that morning and that even though he wasn't waking up now he could still hear me and wanted me to talk to him.

I broke down and cried and pushed away from my mom. I wasn't ready to do this and it took me a few minutes to gain my composure. When I did, I approached my dad's bed and bent over and hugged and kissed him. I whispered in his ear that I was there and I was sorry. I was sorry he was sick. I was sorry he was dying, but most of all I was sorry I didn't go to him that morning.

He survived that day and my aunt took me and my sisters home to get some rest, promising we would be back early in the morning to see him. The next day things were worse; he was no longer making any movements or any sounds. He had faded away even more during the night. We spent the morning just sitting around his bed talking because my mom told us he could hear us and would like to know we were there. Lunch time came and my aunt wanted me and my sisters to go eat, my older sister refused but me and my little sister were told to just go and we would be right back. Again, I got this feeling inside of me that told me something was off, so before leaving the room that time, I went up to my dad, hugged him, and whispered in his ear to wait for me, and he did.

As soon as I got back from lunch, I walked into the room and saw my mom jump up from her chair and put her hands on her mouth. I heard my older sister cry out, "Dad!" with a blood-curdling sob and I looked at my dad and saw that he was struggling. His breathing was labored. I shut my eyes hoping that what I was seeing wasn't real, but when I opened them again, none of it was going away.

I remember sitting in the room after he died: just me, my mom, and my sisters. It was silent. None of us said anything. We just sat there, blank faced and broken. I remember touching my dad's leg and feeling his cold skin and shuddering. There were no words at the time to explain what I felt. Fifteen years later, I still don't have them.

That night, I slept in my dad's bed with a pile of his clothes. I cried into them and screamed, so no one would hear me. The pain was unbearable and I feared I would feel like that forever. The morning after he died, I walked up the stairs and stood outside my mom's bedroom. I could hear her crying and I could hear my older sister crying and telling my mom that she couldn't believe that this was happening. We were all experiencing the same thing, but somehow I felt so far apart from them all.

The funeral was so hard; sitting across from my dad's body was torture. Every moment of my time spent with my dad, good and bad, passed through my mind. Seeing the way my mom was hurting broke me even more, because I hurt so much for her. She had done everything she could to keep my dad healthy and help him beat it and he didn't. You could see it was killing her. I wished then and now that my mom knew and understood how much her efforts, that she gave it her all, meant to us and my dad.

I really saw how my older sister had to take on a big role in the family when it was time to say a final goodbye to my dad at the funeral home. She went up to the casket with my mom and I remember watching her wrap her arm around my mom as she fell apart and comforted her. I was grateful to her in that moment for being exactly what my mom, me and my little sister needed, but I wish I had gotten up and put my arm around her. I bet she needed it, too.

I also noticed how much my little sister didn't understand when I went to the casket with her to say her final goodbye. I said goodbye first and then it was her turn. She said goodbye to him, kissed him, and then looked at me with saddened and confused eyes and asked me why he wasn't waking up. I was shocked She turned to him and told him she wanted him to wake up and I wondered how she would ever be able to understand, when I couldn't understand it myself. My older sister had to become an adult before her time, and my little sister lost some of her innocence. Neither one of them had a choice.

One of the things I thought of a lot in the days after my dad's death was why no one sat me down and told me my dad was going to die. I saw my dad getting worse, but denial sunk in and I didn't believe his time was coming as fast as it had. I wanted someone to pull me out of my denial and tell me the reality of things; but, they didn't. It wasn't until a few nights after my dad's burial that I learned why.

My mom told us that the doctor told my dad that he was going to die three months before he did. The treatment wasn't working and his cancer was spreading fast. When my dad learned the news, he had asked my mom not to tell me and my sisters. He wanted what was left of his life to remain the same and not have me and my sisters behave differently or always look at him with the thought of losing him. I also wondered why he never said anything to us or had a talk with us before he died. Eventually, I realized that he couldn't bring himself to do it. He left his final words with my mom. When my mom told us what he wanted us to know it didn't bring me the peace I thought it would. I think I was looking for something to help my pain but there was nothing. Not even knowing that he came to terms with his destiny.

Saying a final goodbye to my dad changed me in every way. I feel like before my dad was sick, I was a happy kid. I loved to sing and dance and have fun. I was eager to please, because I hated when people were mad at me and I was super-sensitive. But when my dad died, a lot of that changed. I grew angry. I was angry at God for taking my dad; I was angry at my dad for leaving; I was angry at my mom and my sisters and didn't even know why. I was angry at myself. What made it even worse was that my dad's family made the choice to turn their backs on us. Everything I knew about my life was different. I felt like I was losing everything and I hated it. On top of that, I felt so misunderstood. We never had a great relationship with my dad's family. When they turned their back on us, I was so mad at them. I was also sad because I wanted them back, mostly because I just wanted my old life back. No one understood that. I thought my mom was mad at me for missing them and wanting them, I thought my sisters thought I was turning on them because I was taking their side, but I wasn't. I

Chapter Four: The Death of a Parent

knew everything they were doing was wrong and I was so mad at them, but the other half of me was saying it was my dad's family and I needed them. I believed that having them in my life would bring me a piece of my dad when all of him was gone. I know differently now. The pieces of my dad that I was seeking were inside of myself, my sisters and my mom all along.

My mom had a hard time handling her emotions after losing my dad. She shut down completely for a while. She stayed in her room and all she did was cry. I thought I had lost part of my mom while my dad was sick, but after my dad passed, I felt like I lost her completely. A lot of these feelings started with the emotions I never dealt with when my dad was sick and things escalated in my own mind. I was feeling the struggle of my family and myself, but not being able to talk about it made it so much worse. I never learned how to say what I was feeling, because I had shut off for so long. I reached a point in my life where I didn't really care if I died, and I didn't think anyone else would care if I died either. I was spiraling downward and my mom sent me to therapy.

I was seeing a therapist outside of school, as well as at school, because my teachers were concerned about my behaviour. I was spending a lot of time outside of class. I was rude, impatient, and hanging around people that weren't good for me. The therapy didn't work though because I didn't do with it what I was supposed to. I didn't say everything I should have or what they wanted me to and I didn't get better, so I eventually gave up on that. Once my mom got better, she tried to open the line of communication between us, but I rebelled. I started to lie to her about everything. She was smarter than I knew and she saw through all my lies. I was getting into trouble a lot. I realized that I needed to do something, because I was hurting myself and my mom. The first thing I did to make a change was trying to be more open with my mom, but it was so hard for me. Can you imagine being so scared to open up that instead of being able to speak to your mom you have to write it on paper? That's what me and my mom did. At night, we would write letters back and forth to each other and leave them outside each other's door. As we opened up about our feelings, my anger subsided, but it was replaced with guilt.

I came face to face with the reality that I had hurt my mom, which made the time after my dad died even harder. I realized that my older sister had to take on the role of another parent even more after my dad died. She was missing out on so much more of her life. My little sister was suffering with anxiety and I was making everything about myself. I was allowing my anger and sadness to turn me into a horrible person who was not only making my life worse, but theirs too. The guilt was intoxicating; I began to believe that my family was better off without me and wouldn't miss me. I made a decision that I will never be able to forgive myself for. I walked out on my mom and my sisters, I left everything I knew and everyone I loved, and we stopped talking for over a year.

I have changed a lot since those horrible years, but in some ways, I am still the same. I fear that I always will be. Some things leave a mark on you that just doesn't go away. Instead of wanting to die, I fear death. I fear death for myself and all the people I love. Sometimes I think about losing someone else I love and I can't breathe. I can't imagine not having them in my life. I fear being sick or having someone I love be sick. Any little thing becomes a big thing that I need to see the doctor for. I constantly worry about something I am feeling becoming a cancer diagnosis or someone else I know hearing that horrible word. I have two beautiful sons and I fear leaving them behind. I fear getting sick and leaving them with the same feelings I had losing my dad. I can't bear the thought of ever doing that to them.

I worry about not being there to see my sons grow up the same way my dad didn't get to see us grow up. I fear losing my mom and going through the rest of my life without her being by my side. I fear having my husband die and needing to pick up the pieces, or me dying and leaving him to care for my boys. There is still a lot I need to work on, even all these years later. I'm still not the best with my words and my emotions. I sometimes go into a depression and have anxiety attacks and never tell anyone. I just suffer alone and I know I shouldn't.

I will never forget my dad. I think about him every minute of every day. I wonder how much he sees and how much he knows. I speak his name all the time with my mom, my sisters, and my own kids. He lives on in everything we do, because he forever lives in our broken hearts.

Anabia

My name is Anabia and I have three children. Two years ago, my husband died; my son was 9, my middle daughter was 4, and my youngest was 1 and a half. My husband died from a rare form of cancer that was diagnosed quite late. My husband's cancer began in his knee and spread to his spine. By the time it was caught; his nerves and his strength were compromised and he lost most of his locomotor skills and his ability to speak.

I believe that my son could understand what was happening more than my other children, my youngest had a harder time understanding the illness, but I think she could feel what was happening because of me. When we finally received the diagnosis, the children were in school and had just participated in the Terry Fox walk, I think this was the reason my son was so involved and understood so much. Having already started to discuss *cancer* and having seen how a community can come together for it, really gave him some insight into the whole illness. One of my son's first questions was, "Is daddy going to die?" I said that I didn't know. I knew that the illness was severe and that it was probably going to be terminal. So, I started to use the cancer word very freely. I wanted my children to know that this illness is different from the flu, from a typical cold, especially for my girls; they needed to know that this kind of illness is something that can make you very sick. I think there is something profound in children; I believe that they can sense when something is wrong, it is an indescribable understanding that they can connect to. They were so young that the stress this caused them came out as cranky behaviour, lack of sleep, loss of weight, and irregular eating patterns.

My husband was very young when he was diagnosed; he was 30 and it came as a great shock to him and to us. He was very determined, spiritually and emotionally. He was going to hang on to every ounce of life and fight with what he had left in him. He

Chapter Four: The Death of a Parent

would tell the children that he was in pain, but would try to redirect the conversation and the energy. He hated talking about death with the children.

Caring for both the children and my husband was a big step for me; we ended up staying at the hospital for seven days and I was with him 24/7. My mom and my sister were my greatest support system. She would always bring the children whenever he wanted to see them If it was midnight, she would bundle them up and bring them to him. If he could only bare to be around their energy for 10 mins, she would pack them back up and bring them home. She was really amazing for that. There were times when the children would stay with me, I wanted there to be some sort of normalcy, I wanted them to know that we were still a family and that we were doing everything we could to support their dad. I think the fact that my sister is my twin, really helped my youngest; she was able to find comfort in the similarities between my sister and me. There were times that it became so challenging. When my husband couldn't walk anymore, we put all of his stuff in the hallway and a hospital bed in our living room. You could tell that there was someone unhealthy in our home, who was working very hard to get well again.

My children and I are very close. There is a deeper, unspoken, spiritual connection and understanding that we have for one another. I am very comfortable with them, answering their questions and simply just communicating with them every day. My youngest is now 3 and a half. Her brain is so marvelous. I am a strong believer in God, humanity, and the plasticity of the brain. Even though she was so young, she will still recall things that remind her of her father; she will say, *daddy had that* or *daddy used to do that,* and it will be exact.

We pray five times a day as part of our faith, being a Muslim. I told my son to pick a prayer and say it every day for his father; in our religion, we believe that God will give the person you are praying for a message. That is my son's way of remembering his father and keeping him in his every day routine. Often times we will watch videos, look at pictures, we will do many things to keep his memory alive.

We have five prayers in our religion and as a Muslim, from the moment of conception till the moment of death, we work to achieve a higher intellectual level. This world is your time to have a balance between spirituality and the worldliness. Your ultimate goal is to reap enough rewards and to create a ginormous bank account with God full of blessings and good deeds in hopes to attain the highest level of heaven. It's not anywhere. Do good, be good, and say good, this is my mantra with my kids. I say to them, *any time anything can happen.* And we talk about things that happen in nature, because the signs are there for those who want to see. And it's not to fear death, but looking forward to returning to God, because that's where you came from. And to do whatever you can, because you can get the best possible. Just like anything in this world; we want to go to the best universities or colleges; we want to get the best paying jobs, because we want to get somewhere. So spiritually, you want to get somewhere too. It is very much normal and hard any child because cognitively they are not ready to understand the depth or complexity of death. They don't have that special awareness of time. So, for my son, I actually would talk to him about birth, and death, and nature, and things like that. With my daughters, it just happens because they know that daddy is no longer with us and that prayer allows us to remind

Childhood Loss and Grief

ourselves that from God we have come and we will return to him in a state of death when we sleep, and when we wake in the morning and we praise Alah, praising God that he has revived you from a state of death.

There was a stillness after his death and it was very busy in our house. Things changed a whole lot. My sister knew that I would probably benefit from her support, she was quite helpful and she stayed with me. My mom would often come, too. I wasn't really thinking about myself, at all I would say. At any point, it was always about how other people were feeling. There's a certain point when somebody you love deeply is ill, people don't understand that their wants, needs, and desires are top priority. Many people wanted to come visit him, but he didn't want anybody to see him. There's this person's dignity and respect and protecting it was my priority. When your husband dies, there's a 4 month and 10-day period called Edah and it is a dedicated time for grief and mourning. When it started, I thought, *oh my god how is the time going to pass*, and near the end I wished it wouldn't end because people do come and offer you support. You really have to reflect. It's a reflective time about where you are, what you want to do, where you want to go. You should be developing goals for yourself and deciding how are you going to maintain a family and your life. In my case, I wasn't working. I had stopped working when I had my second child and we decided that I would go back to work when the youngest was in full time school. But life changes, so I had to come back to work and deciding where I would work. During this time, we would sit down and if we needed to cry, we would cry and I wouldn't get hysterical but they would ask, *are you sad right now mommy*, and I would say yes and sometimes I would be just sitting and day dreaming or problem solving and they would ask are you sad right now mommy and I'd say no I am just thinking. We visited the cemetery very often. It's a hard concept for children to see and understand, why their daddy is there. Actually, at the funeral, my girls fell asleep and I think that was a blessing because it would have really overwhelmed them if they saw the casket being lowered. I explained to them that they should remember daddy; his body, his soul, his breath, I told them that the soul is like the breath, the shine in your eye; that's with God.

My son was in school, but my girls were not. I would see him off to school and the bus would pick him up, and then he would come home. There were times when he didn't remember things. Every day he would forget things at school, which is not a surprise. I had told his teachers, the day we heard the diagnosis, that he was going to need more support than usual. A social worker got involved, just so he would have an outlet. For the girls, I would talk to them. I would try to do things while being at home with them. My husband wasn't very comfortable if I wasn't in his range of vision. It was very overwhelming for him sometimes, because he knew I would know how to position his pillow, how to help lift him, if he needed to go into a wheelchair or whatever he needed. He was in grade 3 at that time and at that point their school has a system where they stay with the same children and the same teacher every year so his teacher had said to me, 'don't worry a bit, he is a smart child and he is quick with things.' She said you know, don't worry about homework. And there were times where they weren't sure how long this journey would be because it was over a few months, the intense period. I told the school that he would be fatigued sometimes, by the time he got to the hospital in the winter weather downtown from north Brampton, almost Bolton, it would be exhausting. We would be home by 11:00 p.m. and he would have a short sleep, early morning bus ride. I remember the one time where the teacher had tried to say, *he really should be following up with homework*, I said my husband can die any minute and that same night he did. She wasn't trying to be mean but I think she was trying to have that same sort of higher level of expectation so that he would be meeting some of the other typical children. A week or so after my husband's death, my son was attending school. I think he missed a total of 10 days which is impressive considering the intensity of what we were going through. He was able to recover and continue on; we had a lot of transitions the year he died. Teachers in the school were not aware how to approach this although, they were very empathetic and compassionate; they want to be supportive but I think it would be helpful. Children also don't know how to deal with this because they haven't learned it at home. Shad told them to just say I'm sorry this happened, and that sometimes he might need to cry and that's okay. He said he was scared to go because they were in a portable at that time. I took him to school that day and I said I will be here with you if you want me to open the door for you or come in but he was a brave little guy, he said *no, I will be ok* and he walked to the steps. It's overwhelming. You suddenly feel like everybody is staring at you. My side of the family knows a lot of people so we had many different people in our house, coming and going at any given time and he saw the full impact in his consciousness about how many people our side knows. The school was supportive and I hadn't told him this but I had already known that his social worker was a blessing too, she was a cancer survivor. She had a different level of understanding. One thing she said, was 'whatever you are doing with him, keep doing it because it's working' and that was really humbling for me.

My son actually said to me, "Mom I don't want you to get married again." I said that's fine, I'm glad you shared that with me. I told him that it isn't something in my horizon, it is not one of my goals. I said, sometimes things happen even if we say never, we don't always know what will be in your future. We believe very firmly that whatever happens, it is your fait and destiny that are predetermined for you and there are different paths you can take that will lead you to that destination. My firm belief is that whatever happens in your life even if it seems horrible and challenging and difficult, there's always a blessing. I pray to Alah that I will be shown the blessing in this and will come to know, and understand the true meaning. The younger ones are curious about this. My middle one would do a lot of play, and acting out; roleplaying. Her and the little one, because her language skills are so developed, they would play mommy and daddy and they would use terms of endearment that me and my husband would exchange, sometimes one would pretend to be the daddy and the other the mommy or the child. They want to know what time I am coming home, what I am doing, when I will be coming back.

Our family has changed and is different from other families now. Everybody's family is different but your family is different because daddy is not here anymore. Mommy has to work which means mommy is not home as much. We talk about some of the things mommy does inside and outside the home and then we talk about some of the things that they do and what their responsibilities are. My son has chores in the home, to gather all the garbage and the recycling and to put it out. If something is not in its place it needs to be put away or there are consequences. Buying groceries, doing the laundry, folding the laundry, putting it away, whatever they are able to manage. They know they have responsibilities and they have things to do. Simple things like your shoes have to be on the mat. Things that are self-help skills. I am very big on that and life skills. I have always been that way so it's just more heightened because that's just the way life is.

I have concerns for my son particularly, because on occasion he does get really bad headaches and that was part of my husband's life since we met. We weren't quite sure what that was from. We thought it was just with the pressure, how people get migraines and stuff. So, on occasion when he gets headaches or if he has leg or knee pain, he is intensely afraid that it can be something serious. He is like his dad; he doesn't like hospitals or doctors; he can't stomach the sight of blood. It's a challenge. He's only gotten one blood test done in his life and I think that's a good thing. My concern would be that when he's a little bit older and he's god willing, healthy and moving along in his life and he comes to his late 30s like his did, will he feel like he is going to become ill. On Father's Day, I know it's hard for them, especially my son. His friends have said, *I'm sorry about your dad, I feel sorry for you.* They are trying to be empathetic; they really don't know how to go about it and it's awkward for them. I always tell them that parent's day is every day because you make that prayer; you make that gift every day. Last year we went to Gilda's Club which is a bereavement centre and I took them purposely because I wanted them to see other children who were going through or had gone through and they really enjoyed that.

I relied on my spirituality. If you have any sort of spirituality or spiritual belief, be mindful of that and take it one day at a time. You really have to take some dedicated time to mourn and to talk about it, feel it, experience it. I am a firm believer in us being very sensory. You have to cry it out, you have to talk it out, you have to hear it out. Hear your own voice or hear other people's stories. You have to write it out sometimes in a journal. It feels like you have exhaled. If you need to go and visit the cemetery, it will be helpful. I think the thing that helped me, being a Muslim widow was that dedicated time. And you need that time. I believe there are certain things in our faith that we do, that we don't understand but afterwards we come to know. I am really blessed and humbled that I am at peace with the way his life journey ended because I know I did whatever I could. I left no stone unturned in whatever I could, whatever networking I could do, whatever consult I could get, whatever it was I made that effort. Give the other person dignity and give yourself dignity and tell yourself it's okay; you did the best that you could do in that circumstance and you will continue to do your best. Take one step at a time, one day at time. Thinking a few years down the road can be very daunting and overwhelming at the best of times, at most, think 3-6 months in advance if that. You know, surviving to the weekend is probably best or surviving to the middle of the week. Every day, every week as it goes by, you know, eventually you will come to know it and attempt to have a positive perspective. Even on the best of times having that hope uplifts you psychologically, mentally, spiritually, emotionally, and physically. Look for the blessings.

Chapter Four: The Death of a Parent

Mariam

My name is Mariam and I have three children. When they were young, they lost their father and I lost my husband. My daughter was seven, my son was five, and my youngest son had just turned four. Today, they are sixteen, fifteen, and thirteen.

My husband's death came to us as a surprise. He came home from work, ate dinner, and went to sleep, a very typical kind of night. He woke up at midnight and couldn't breathe, we called 911 and they announced he was having a heart attack. I was with him in the ambulance where he lost his ability to speak. I waited two hours before seeing him once he was in the emergency room. Then we received the news; he stopped breathing and had gone into a coma after they resuscitated him, for three days he was brain dead in a coma, and then he died.

My husband was a pharmacist; he was healthy and maintained his yearly check-ups, nothing ever came up. At the hospital, we were made aware that he had been suffering from type 2 diabetes and blood pressure; his arteries were 90% blocked. This was such a shock for me, *how could we not have known that he was suffering for more than two years*, he never showed any symptoms; I thought I knew about diabetes.

Once receiving this news, I started to blame myself. I was the one who cooked every day, was it something I did? So many thoughts were going through my mind. As a Muslim, we believe that when it is your time then you must go, the story that goes along with it, is something we use to cope and comfort ourselves; however, I just couldn't believe that this wasn't caught, how could we have missed this?

It was hard to help my children understand what was happening. My in-laws were taking care of them when this happened; they kept asking where I was; I stayed in the hospital with him for as long as he would be there. I did not leave, I couldn't. The only contact I had with my children was through the phone, they kept asking *where he was*, I just kept telling them *he was sick and that he would be coming home soon*.

I remember being so afraid to face my children and tell them what had just happened. I had to compose myself, in the best way I could, and try to figure out how to tell my children that their father had just passed away. I pushed forward, and moved onto making arrangements for the funeral, during this time my mother in law told my children. When I finally got to see them, that night, we just hugged and cried. I don't even know for how long, we just cried.

I don't think they quite understood, or comprehended, what exactly it meant to lose their father. They couldn't believe it, "Is it true? Did he die? Are we never going to see him again?." I really tried to answer them, but it was so hard. My four-year-old, he could not fully grasp what was happening. He would see his father's clothing around the house and ask why *it* is there, but why *he* wasn't. It was extremely hard to answer his questions and try to put the pieces together for him, he was so young; he just couldn't understand why his father was no longer with us, it didn't make sense.

After my husband's passing, my children and I lived with my in-laws for the duration of the Islamic mourning period; four months and ten days. This time brought me and my children together and our relationship strengthened. Although, during this period my father became ill and I was forced to make a decision between staying and going to visit him – I went in view of the fact that life can be taken so quickly. I had to go alone; my in-laws refused to let my children come with me. The plan was that I would go for a month, when I got there my family expressed their unpleasant view of my in-laws and did not want me to return home. My passport was taken from me along with any control that I had over my own life. I was in Kenya, scared and hopeless. I was forced to be without my children for a year and half; I could not beg or plead, I had no assistance in getting back home. I found access to the internet and quickly came in contact with my family for help. I fought for my freedom and was able to return home.

After this incident, my in-laws tried to take custody of my children; they claimed that I had abandoned them. They [in-laws] had taken over my home, I had nothing when I arrived back in Canada. The first thing I had to do was reach my children; when I finally got to them, my in-laws would not let me in the house. I stood outside, looking at my children through the window, crying and weeping. I tried to come to an agreement with my in-laws. They said if I took my children they would call 911 and claim it as kidnapping, because they now had custody. I had no idea what the *rules* were, I had only been in Canada for three years and with my husband gone, I had no one to guide me. I went to stay at a women's shelter where I received legal help. I was eventually able to regain custody of my children; I was able to live and breathe again, to protect and build my family all over again.

Unfortunately, this took a toll on my children. Not only did they lose their father, but also for what must have felt like forever, they were missing their mother. After a few months of me being gone, I was able to have monitored phone calls with them, they would ask *when I was coming back,* all I was ever allowed to say was *soon.* My youngest son was the most affected by this situation. Every time I left the house, for about seven months, he would ask if I were going to come back home, 'Please come back!' he would say. He couldn't understand that I was going to stay. My middle son, he would break down. Every once in a while, he would just cry, about his father and everything that had happened. He tried to take on the father role, even today he is always checking in with me, asking me where I am going, when I'll be back. He is strong, with his siblings and with me. My oldest, she took over the parent role for my boys. It affected her the most. She began to have anxiety attacks; at home, at school. I was broken for her, I had no idea what this was, I felt helpless and responsible. I began taking her to a psychotherapist. She has been getting treatment for about five years now and her anxiety has improved; it is less frequent now. There are still triggers to her anxiety but she has learned how to process them.

Our relationship after this only grew stronger. On one hand, they would tell me that they *always knew I was going to come back,* but emotionally they needed time to open back up to me. They needed to trust me again. They started to open up about how they were feeling, after some time. We are inseparable now; we are so happy; they are so happy.

After the passing of their father, my children changed. My daughter became more mature, before she should have ever had to. She started taking on more responsibility and acted as a caregiver towards her brother. She even took on the responsibility of ensuring that I was in good spirits, she would reassure me that everything was going to be okay; 'Were going to make it through this...We'll be okay.' These were stressors that no child should have to face, but she did, and she did it with compassion and grace.

My middle child became very reserved. He is precautious of the people he lets into his life. In school, while I was gone, he wouldn't eat or speak. He even passed out in his class once. I think the stress of what was going on his life came out emotionally and physically, this has shaped a great amount of who he is today.

My youngest, I don't know if he changed much. He was so young when he lost his father. He would joke and laugh; he does not do this as much anymore, but he's still there. In school, they would say that he would have outburst and tremble; he has a lot of anger inside of him. He's learning to cope with his outbursts; he is learning to talk when something is bothering him and he is good at it, he will come home and tell me everything.

My children are so close to each other. They are there for one another and communicate with each other all the time; their bonds really deepened.

It was mostly just us four against the world after all of this. We didn't have much support aside from my friends. When I came back from Kenya I actually stayed with this friend before my time at the women's shelter. She has always been a support for me, I knew I wasn't alone. Spiritually, my children and I have always found comfort and guidance in God. Our [my children and my] strength comes from religion and love.

I allow my children to see their grandparents when they like to for a few hours, every few months. They have cousins that they are close to, I don't want my children to lose any more family. I believe that everything is pre-ordained and happens for a reason; when I cannot see the good in things, I know eventually I will understand why it happened. Ultimately, my children are everything to me.

I am truly blessed and grateful to see how much my children have grown. They do not fear living their lives, they are always hopeful for the future. I am so proud of them. I talk to them a lot and try to provide guidance. If they want or need something and I am in a position to provide, I try my best to always sustain them. If not, we collaborate on how to get it; we sit down, set a goal, and make a plan to achieve it. It is so important – to me – to keep our communication open so they don't lose sight of themselves.

We talk about their father a lot. I think it comes up at different times when you would least expect it. When my daughter turned sixteen she started to cry, realizing her father would not see any of her milestones. These are the moments that sting a little more. We cry and we talk about it and although nothing can make it *better,* we all know that there is a part of him in us, forever.

Although, my in-laws took majority of his belongings after he passed, I managed to keep three watches; one for each of my children to have in memory of their father. We treasure the home that we had together, when it was all of us, we still live there today. We donate in his name and pray that he gets the blessings for it. Whenever we remember him, we pray for him and for a good after life.

Holding on to my faith, very tightly, helped me through these challenging years. Believing that everything would eventually be right again. It's not easy to lose someone, by any means, I had to struggle and rebuild; while believing that everything would fall into place. It has taken a very long time to be in a place where I can honestly say, I am happy. I will never stop missing my husband, but he is with me through everything I do and although he is gone, he is never forgotten.

Sandra and Caroline (Written by Dr. Elena Merenda)

Sandra was approximately 2 years old when she lost her father. She is now twenty-two years old, and recalls very little about him. Her memories, she explained, are a picture painted by her mother, her brother, and pictures and videos of her father. Sandra's father was a person with a very complicated mental health history. Sandra's mother, Caroline, explained that he struggled with addiction for a long time. Sandra's father ended up killing himself after being declared clear minded by his doctor. This happened around a time when mental illness was quite understated and not much was known about its effects. Caroline suggested that the procedures and treatments her husband received were based on the little knowledge doctors had on mental health and illness and therefore couldn't him.

Sandra knew from a very young age that her father died. Sandra was a toddler when he died; therefore, the grieving process was different for her. Caroline recalls that Sandra did not have an immediate reaction to her father's death. She said, *"There was nothing coming from her at all"* which made quite the contrast when compare to her older brother's reaction. Sandra's brother is a year older than her and Caroline remembers his reaction when their father passed. He asked questions about him, and wanted to know when he would come back. Sandra explained her own reaction similarly to her mom's memories: "…she read me stories about death but, for me, and for my brother too, we never really…acknowledged it. It was just kind of like we went on with our lives because, for me…in that developmental stage where it was just kind of like there was a person there, I knew who he was, but I didn't necessarily have that immediate connection because he was there for such a short period of my life."

Caroline, her mother tried to keep her children connected to their father by showing them videos and talking about him. Caroline said, "So, for a while on Father's Day, or his birthday, we would make cards and then go and visit the cemetery. This was just when they were young. It pretty much stopped, I'm going to say at the age of 10. Then once in a while maybe it was once a year, and then once they got older it was less, once every 2 years, we would go to the cemetery." Caroline tried to keep the memory of their father by starting traditions and allowing the children to be part of those traditions. However, when it came to talking about the details surrounding his death the communication fell short.

Sandra began to question her father's death when she was in sixth grade. She knew he was dead, but she began to wonder how he died. She never imagined that her father committed suicide. She always assumed that he died from cancer because Sandra battled cancer a few years after her dad died. But as she grew older, she realized, "…cancer isn't contagious. I didn't get sick because he gave me cancer. So if he didn't die from cancer, how did he die?"

When she learned of her father's suicide, Sandra went through a time of turmoil while attempting to come to terms with the news. She was heavily impacted by her mother's silence in the matter. In Caroline's mind, what she had done was the best she could do. Caroline never talked about how Sandra's father died, and even if she curious Sandra never asked her. Sandra found out about his suicide when she was visiting family. She struggled processing this new information since she never imagined suicide as the cause of her father's death and much less being told by a family member that was not her mother. She felt very disappointed and angry that it was not her mother telling her this. As she reflects upon what happened she says "I guess I didn't like it that it happened so much later in life, where I think it could have helped me out early on to identify more with myself in my family because there is that division." However, she understands that for Caroline it was hard to raise two children while grieving the loss of a spouse. Caroline mentioned that she struggled quite a bit after Sandra's father died. She said, "Then all of a sudden, he died, and I had to rely on you know, not just family, which I did a lot, but friends and professionals, which was a new world for me."

Tara (Written by Dr. Elena Merenda)

Tara was only 15 years old when she met Eric and her whole life changed. It was love at first sight. After only dating for a couple of weeks, they were married. One year later, Tara gave birth to their beautiful son Jacob.

Before they got married, Tara knew that Eric enjoyed to drink alcohol. She was okay with that though, because he was in control of his habit. Once Jacob was born, however, Eric's habit quickly turned into a dangerous addiction. Eric was an alcoholic and he physically abused Tara. Eric's addiction and abuse towards Tara increased over the next 7 years. Tara threatened to leave Eric every day, but something kept her there. When Jacob turned 7, Eric promised to change his ways. He promised to get sober and insisted that another child would strengthen their relationship. One year later, Sally was born. "They wanted to have me so they could prove that they could have a happier family, maybe things could change, but it didn't end up that way." Eric's addiction to alcohol and the domestic violence continued.

One night, when Sally was only 4 years old, Eric came home really drunk. Eric and Tara were fighting and it quickly escalated out of control. Eric took Sally out of bed and onto the balcony. He was shaking her over the railing, threatening to throw Sally over the edge. That's when Tara decided that she couldn't risk her children's safety for another day, and she filed for divorce. After the separation, Jacob chose to live with their father and Sally lived with her mother. Between the ages of four and eight, Sally maintained contact with her father, as she saw him every weekend.

When Sally turned eight, she and her mother moved from Turkey to Canada where many of her maternal family resided. At the age of nine, only a year after their arrival in Canada, Sally lost her father to a traffic accident. She was devastated and shocked, and worried for her brother who was still in Turkey. "My reaction was just

Childhood Loss and Grief

nothing...I was just shocked for a while." The period of shock and denial lasted about 3 to 4 years. ."..every time a stranger approached me 'Oh where is your dad?', that was the time when it would hit me. That was the time when I would realize 'oh my father is gone' and I have to tell them 'oh he passed away'."

After losing her father, Sally claims that she tried to uphold a strong character in front of her peers; trying to show them that her father's death didn't affect her. "I didn't want people to feel bad for me, so I wanted to get over it and I wanted to act like, 'oh like, oh guys its fine you know, my mom and dad divorced when I was four so it doesn't really affect me'...I didn't want to show anyone I was weak or anything, but I was actually weak and I would cry at home to my mom."

Before the death of her father, Sally said that she was a happy, silly and energetic child; which she observed in her home videos. "I watched other videos of me when I was ten or eleven. I look more calm, more mature...it looked like I acted cold with my family. I think I wanted to put that boundary or reminder to myself ever since my father's death, like never be too close or attached to someone because they could leave anytime...."

Sometime after their father's death, Jacob spent six months in Canada. He expressed envy towards Sally, which continues to this day. He continuously tells Sally that she doesn't know how it feels to be him; having to lose a father without support from a mom and being there in Turkey witnessing their father's death alone. He claims that he struggled more than she did because their mom was always there as a support for Sally, but not for him. He claims that Sally is weak and he does not express much love towards her anymore. Sally remembers her brother's love for her during her childhood; he would protect her, take care of her, and save his money to buy her toys. She claims that their relationship weakened after their father's death. "...he would have that hate towards my mom...he thought that if my mom didn't leave my father everything would've been perfect, we would've been a perfect family." Sally, on the other hand, always supported her mother's decision to divorce her father. "...it's not because I grew up with her" she claims, it's because Tara divorced Eric to protect herself and her children. Tara didn't want her children to witness any more domestic violence because she cared for the well-being of her children.

After her father's death, Sally was like a best friend to her mom. She focused on her mother's emotions rather than on her own. When Tara cried, Sally would support her and try her best to prevent her mother from crying. Sally didn't want to be selfish in expressing her own grief and she didn't want to show signs of blame for her mother taking her away from her father. The death of her father was not her mother's fault and Sally believed that her mother was also impacted by her father's death.

All her life, Sally has been attributed by statements similar to, "You lost your dad when you were young, what do you even remember about him?." She puts forth that just because she was nine, it doesn't mean she doesn't remember her father, her moments with him, and what she has been through. Her memories have all created a scar which still haven't healed and may not ever heal. Three years ago, when Sally was 17 years old, she was on the subway going to school. She smelled a scent that reminded her of her father and when she looked back it was a person who appeared to be homeless and drunk. She was shocked by the trigger that brought back the memories of her father. She was only four when she last witnessed her father drunk. Despite the young age, she remembered it. "So an alcoholic made me remember my father...Imagine, a four-year-old remembered...the scent. You know I still can't believe that." That's when she realized that there will always be something that will trigger her memory of her father.

About a year ago, Tara decided to marry and now lives with her husband in Turkey. During the time of her mother's remarriage, Sally was very concerned about who her step-father was. "I didn't want my mom to go through any pain that she did before. So, I was searching about this guy, I was like, 'where is he, how old is he, how many kids does he have, why did he divorced from his other wife like what was the problem, would my mom be unhappy?' I was more concerned about my mom's happiness than me being selfish like 'no I can't let go of my mom'. It was more like 'my mom needs to be happy, she deserves it'." As Sally is currently engaged and is planning her marriage, she is concerned for her future family as she fears the possibility of divorcing her future-husband. She says "I wouldn't want my own children to feel how I felt because it's not an easy thing." Although the loss she experienced of her father through divorce and death occurred years ago, it seems that her experiences are haunting her as she takes steps towards big decisions in life.

CHAPTER 5

Divorce

Source: Creative Commons

"When my dad divorced my mom, it was kind of like him leaving me also."
-Nicole Richie

According to a report from the Vanier Institute of the Family (2011), 4 in 10 first marriages end in divorce (as cited in Wilson, 2014). ***Divorce*** can be defined as the reconstruction of the family (White, Martin, Bartolic, 2013). It is a process that involves loss, grief, anger, endings, and new familial patterns and traditions (Wilson, 2014).

Research suggests that both children and adults are impacted by divorce. Children of divorced parents, when compared to children of married parents, scored lower on social, emotional, health, and academic outcomes. The negative effect of divorce on children continues into their adulthood. Adult children of divorced parents are more likely to attain less education, have lower psychological well-being, have trouble in their own marriages, and have a higher chance of divorce in their own marriage (White, Martin, Bartolic, 2013). Just like any loss, with divorce comes grief. During divorce, children lose a parent in the home, they lose the stability that came with a two parent family, sometimes they lose the home they grew up in, and often, with a move in houses comes a move in schools. Therefore, the end of a marriage may trigger a variety of reactions for parents and children including: denial, anger, depression, and acceptance. (Brand, 2018).

STAGES OF GRIEF WHEN PARENTS DIVORCE

When parents get divorced, children experience the stages of grief.

Shock and Denial

Children have a family life that, to them, is "normal." During divorce or separation, children first experience shock and denial stage. During this stage, children have to work to understand the divorce and what is going to happen as a result of the divorce (White, Martin, Bartolic, 2013).

Anger

Next children move into a stage of anger. This is a normal reaction to divorce and children need time to work through their anger and guilt. Sometimes, children pick one parent to be mad at and not at the other parent (White, Martin, Bartolic, 2013).

Depression

When children sense that their life is falling apart, they may withdraw and feel sad and detached from their family and friends (White, Martin, Bartolic, 2013).

Chapter Five: Divorce

Dialogue and Bargaining

When children move into the dialogue and bargaining stage, they make efforts to get the family back together. They will fantasize about reconciliation and will promise to be good if their parents will just reconsider their decision to divorce. Children may even develop ways such as being sick or getting into trouble at school, to get their parents together. This is how children work through the guilt of feeling that they were the reason for the divorce. It is also part of accepting the permanence of the divorce (White, Martin, Bartolic, 2013).

Acceptance

Reaching the acceptance stage means that the child has adjusted to the reality and permanence of the divorce. It usually also means that they are ready to be vulnerable and open themselves to love again. The entire grief process involves loss and requires that children overcome feelings of rejection, humiliation, unlovability, and powerlessness (White, Martin, Bartolic, 2013).

Numerous longitudinal studies have investigated the short and long term effects of divorce on children (Amato, 1991; Amato, 1988; Barber & Eccles, 1992; Hess & Camara, 1979). According to these studies, the initial period of separation is stressful for children because it is unexpected. Since most children are unaware of the complicated issues in their parents' marriage, a large number of children react with intense sense of shock, disbelief, distress, sorrow, anxiety, and anger. Developmental factors affect how children manifest this distress. For example, preschool children experience regression, anxiety, fears and neediness, sleep disturbances, and increased aggression. School-aged children experience anxiety, loneliness, and a sense of powerlessness. They may also feel responsible for the divorce, they are conflicted about choosing sides, and they have fantasies about reconciliation. Their performance in school and their peer relationships might also be negatively affected (Amato, 1991; Amato, 1988; Barber & Eccles, 1992; Hess & Camara, 1979).

SHORT-TERM EFFECTS OF DIVORCE ON CHILDREN

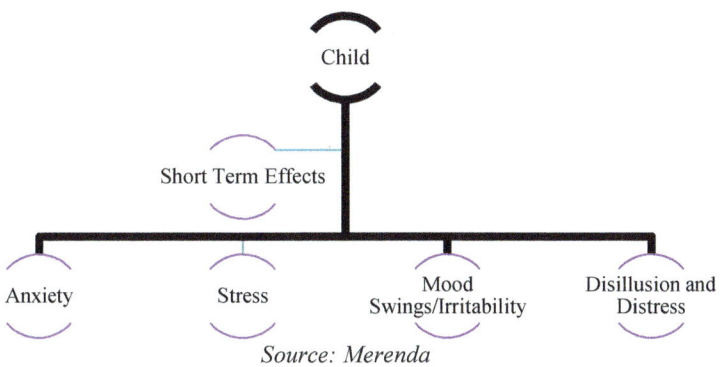

Source: Merenda

Anxiety

The process and the aftermath of divorce causes children to become nervous and anxious. Younger children are more prone anxiety than older children because they are more dependent on their parents. An anxious school-age child will have difficulty concentrating at school and a younger anxious child may lose interest in play-based activities that he/she once found exciting (White, Martin, Bartolic, 2013).

Stress

Depending on their age, some children falsely consider themselves the reason behind their parents' divorce and assume the responsibility to fix the relationship. This is a great responsibility, with several repercussions like negative thoughts and nightmares (White, Martin, Bartolic, 2013).

Mood Swings and Irritability

Young children may suffer from mood swings and irritability. Some children will withdraw, preferring to spend time alone (White, Martin, Bartolic, 2013).

Disillusion and Distress

Children of divorce may feel hopeless and disillusioned due to the lack of emotional support from their parents. This situation can become worse if the child is looked after by a single parent with no access to the other parent (White, Martin, Bartolic, 2013).

Short-term effects of divorce can impede on a child's psychological and physiological well-being and development, which can have long-term implications on the child.

LONG-TERM EFFECTS OF DIVORCE ON CHILDREN

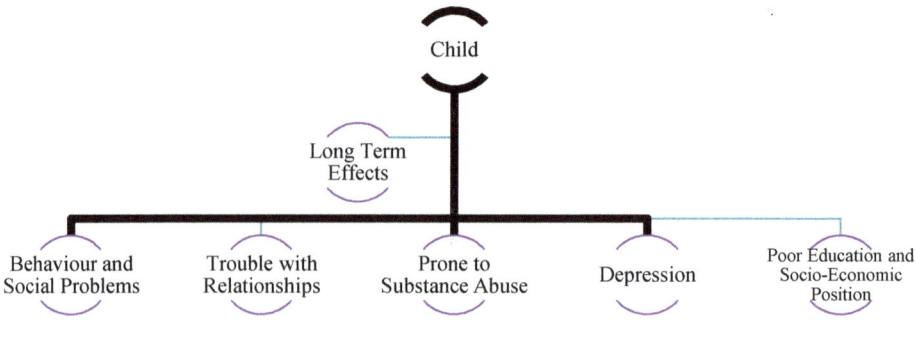

Source: Merenda

Behavioural and Social Problems

Children from divorced families are at a greater risk of developing violent and antisocial behaviour. Sometimes, these behavioural and social problems may lead to the development of a criminal mindset, especially during the adolescent years. Studies suggest that most children of divorce display aggression and disobedience and in extreme cases, children become a social oddity (White, Martin, Bartolic, 2013).

Difficulty with Relationships

When children grow up observing a marriage fail, they develop doubts about love and marriage. They have trust issues and find it challenging to resolve conflicts in a relationship (White, Martin, Bartolic, 2013).

Prone to Substance Abuse

Research demonstrates a higher incidence of substance abuse in teens whose parents are divorced. There are other factors that determine the adolescent's tendency to use drugs and harmful substances, such as the care provided by the single parent; however, the probability of an adolescent surrendering to the temptation is high (White, Martin, Bartolic, 2013).

Depression

The pain and distress on children caused by parents' divorce can cause depression. Children who witness divorce have a higher incidence of depression and social withdrawal. Research suggests that divorce can be a contributing factor in cases of bipolar disorder (White, Martin, Bartolic, 2013).

Poor Education and Socio-Economic Position

Children who experience divorce show a drastic drop in their school grades. It can significantly impede a child's ability to learn. A decrease in educational progress can limit career options for the child as an adult, which make it difficult to have a decent socio-economic status (White, Martin, Bartolic, 2013).

In regards to long-term effects, children of divorce are significantly more likely to have externalizing problems including conduct disorder and antisocial behaviours; relationship problems with peers, parents, authority figures; and academic problems. They are also more likely to have internalizing symptoms such as depression, anxiety and low self-esteem (Martin, Volkmar, Lewis, 2007).

CHILDREN IN DIVORCED AND NON-DIVORCED FAMILIES

Research on the functioning of children from divorced families has been compared to the functioning of children from non-divorced families. These comparisons suggest

Childhood Loss and Grief

that children from divorced families have more behavioural, emotional, health, and academic problems. Compared with children in non-divorced families, children from divorced families are more likely to have conduct problems, lower academic achievement, more social difficulties, poorer self-esteem, and they show signs of psychological maladjustment (Clarke-Stewart & Brentano, 2006; Furstenberg & Cherlin, 1991).

Furthermore, children from divorced families experience emotions such as "embarrassment, fear of abandonment, grief over loss, irrational hope of reconciliation, worry about their parents' well-being, anxiety about divided loyalties, and uncertainty about romantic relationships" (Clarke-Stewart & Brentano, 2006, p. 108).

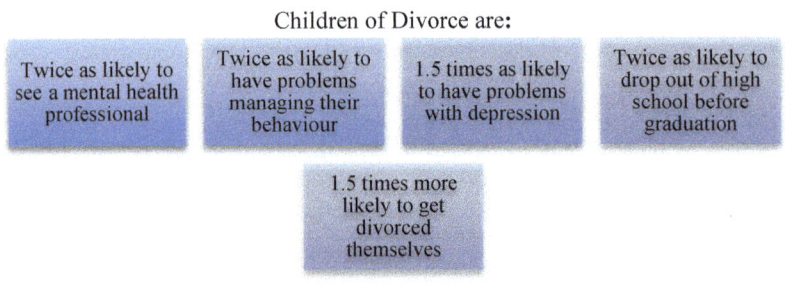

Source: Emery, 2004

High conflict marriages followed by high conflict divorce situations have a negative influence on the psychological adjustment of children. However, the psychological impact of divorce on children is dependent on a number of risk and protective factors. Protective factors include a strong relationship with at least one parent, parental warmth, and the support of siblings and peers. Some studies indicate that the parent and child's gender also influences a child's adjustment to divorce. Boys are more vulnerable than girls to have both long-term and short-term effects. In families where the mother has custody, boys may have improved adjustment with regular paternal contact (Martin, Volkmar, Lewis, 2007).

Children's Reaction to Divorce at Different Ages and Stages

Every child has a unique reaction to divorce. In general, children experience feelings of confusion, betrayal, and neglect. However, children's reactions to their parents' divorce varies with age and depends on their personality and temperament, the family's history, and the support they receive from their circle of friends, school, and community (Clarke-Stewart & Brentano, 2006; Furstenberg & Cherlin, 1991).

Infants and Toddlers

It is easy to assume that divorce does not affect babies, especially those who have not yet developed an emotional attachment to the parent leaving the home. However, infants are vulnerable because their ability to thrive and survive is influenced by their environment. Infants attach to their caregivers and depend on them for their physical and emotional needs. Through those relationships, they establish confidence in the world around them in order to build a strong foundation for mastering developmental milestones (Clarke-Stewart & Brentano, 2006). A child's experiences and relationships during infancy lay the foundation for what he/she think about himself/herself and others. Distrust begins when the infant learns that crying does not have an effect. The infant believes that he/she is powerless and if calls go unanswered long enough, the infant learns to feel unsafe, unprotected, and helpless (Wallerstein & Blakeslee, 2003).

Although infants and toddlers have a limited understanding of their world and they cannot understand the process of divorce, infants and toddlers will feel when parents are upset and are in conflict, and they will react to this. They imitate adult facial expressions at the age of two months. A breast feeding infant might turn his/her gaze away from the breast, refusing to feed or sleep. A toddler might rock in a chair, bang his/her head, or cling to the parent.

Infants and toddlers need predictable caregiving and routines. Often, infants who have regular overnight visits with their father are more insecure and disorganized in their attachment to their mothers and fathers, they are less positive, less affectionate, and less engaged with their parents, in comparison to children from non-divorced families (Clarke-Stewart & Brentano, 2006).

Common Effects of Divorce for Infants and Toddlers

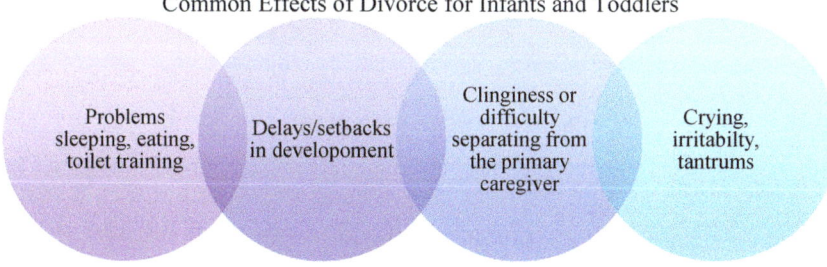

Source: Merenda

Preschoolers

Preschool children are egocentric and see themselves as the centre of the universe. They believe that they have control over or are the cause of what happens around them. Along with their egocentrism and their limited understanding of divorce, preschoolers might believe that the divorce is their fault. They may believe that they caused the change in their family and the sadness they feel around them (Clarke-Stewart & Brentano, 2006).

At this age, children are developing a separate relationship with each of their parents and they conceptualize these relationships in terms of the person's physical presence. For preschoolers, love is being with the person; therefore, when a parent leaves the home, preschool children may believe that mom or dad is leaving *them*.

The child's sense that the world is a secure place where all his/her needs will be met is impacted by the divorce; therefore, when the parent leaves, preschool children are frightened. They are afraid of being alone and abandoned (Clarke-Stewart & Brentano, 2006).

At this stage, children can adapt to changes to their physical and social environment, but they still need predictability. Compared with older or younger children, preschoolers are most distressed and upset, most vulnerable to feelings of loss and rejection, and they have the most intense reaction to divorce because they cannot tell the different between what's real and what's imaginary (Clarke-Stewart & Brentano, 2006).

Surprisingly, preschool children's reaction to divorce is like their reaction to the death of a parent. They experience stress, guilt, loneliness, and sadness.

Common Effects of Divorce for Preschoolers

- Fear of being abandoned by one or both parents
- Delays/setbacks in development
- Clinginess, emotionally needy behaviour OR withdrawal
- Increased anger, crying, tantrums
- Physical complaints (headaches, stomach aches)

Source: Merenda

School-aged Children

School-age children understand what the word "divorce" means, but they may still be just as surprised and worried as younger children when their parents decide to divorce. Children at this age can think more abstractly; they may feel sad and worry about the future. They may worry about where they will live, who will take care of them, and how their place and role in the family will change. They may also have fantasies about their parents getting back together (Clarke-Stewart & Brentano, 2006).

Understanding does not relieve the children's pain or anxiety. School-age children experience grief and sadness. They long for their intact family and yearn for the lost parent. School-age children's most common reaction is anger. They blame one parent for the divorce and for the other parent's suffering, and they openly express their animosity and hatred (Clarke-Stewart & Brentano, 2006).

Furthermore, school-aged children often have problems in school. Children of divorce are more likely to have lower grades; perform worse on reading, spelling, and math tests; have less regular school attendance; less popular and socially competent; more aggressive and disobedient; and lack self-control (Clarke-Stewart & Brentano, 2006).

Chapter Five: Divorce

Common Effects of Divorce for School-Agers

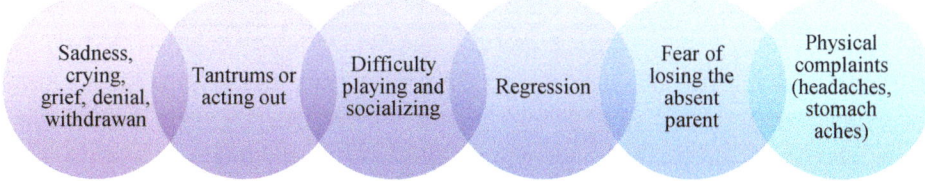

Source: Merenda

PERSPECTIVES ON DIVORCE

A number of perspectives propose an explanation for why divorce might have negative effects on children's lives. Most theories focus on three notions: parental absence, economic disadvantage, and family conflict (Amato & Kieth, 1991).

Parental Absence Perspective

The family is the most influential and important factor in the socialization of young children. There is a traditional notion that two-parent families with both parents living in the same household as the children are better, more nurturing environments for children's development than the single-parent family. Consequently, the negative effects of divorce on children are often credited to socialization deficits, as a result of growing up with only one parent in the household (Amato & Kieth, 1991).

Divorce leads to a decrease in the quantity and quality of contact between children and the parent who lives outside of the home, especially if that parent works and is constrained in the amount of time and energy he/she has to spend with the child. As a result, children of divorce often experience less parental attention, help, and supervision. This decline in parental support and modelling may increase the likelihood of academic failure, low self-esteem, misbehaviour, and inadequate social skills (Amato & Kieth, 1991).

A parental absence perspective on the negative effects divorce has on children leads to the following hypotheses. First, children who experience the death of a parent experience problems similar to those of children who experience parental divorce. Second, since a stepparent can provide an alternative role model and source of support for children, children of divorce have fewer problems if the parent who moved out of the home remarries. Third, disruptive effects of living in a single-parent family are partly lessened if the parents who moved out of the home maintain close relationships with their children. In summary, the frequency and quality of contact with the parent who moves out of the home is positively associated with children's well-being (Amato & Kieth, 1991).

93

Economic Disadvantage Perspective

The economic disadvantage perspective assumes that economic hardship is responsible for the negative effects divorce has on children. Divorce can potentially lead to a decline in the standard of living for single-parent families. Economic hardship may negatively affect children's nutrition, health, and academic success, as single parents are unable to afford resource such as tutoring, educational toys, books, and computers.

Furthermore, limited means may also lead families to live in low socioeconomic neighborhoods in which school programs are poorly financed and services are inadequate (Amato & Kieth, 1991).

This perspective hypothesizes that children's well-being is enhanced during divorce if the parent they live with remarries, because this usually results in improvements in financial status. This perspective also suggests that children experience fewer problems if fathers have custody, because fathers generally earn more income than do mothers (Amato & Kieth, 1991).

Family Conflict Perspective

The family conflict perspective assumes that conflict between parents before and during the separation period is a stressor for children. Conflict between parents creates a negative home environment in which children experience stress, unhappiness, and insecurity. Unfortunately, children tend to be drawn into their parents' conflict, impacting parent-child relations. Studies have indicated that conflict in the home has a negative impact on children's psychological adjustment because conflict is likely to stress parents and make them less effective in caring for their children (Amato & Kieth, 1991).

Chapter Five: Divorce

A Case Study

Vanessa

My name is Vanessa and I am currently 25 years old. At the age of 10, my mom and dad separated. I can clearly remember the moment it happened. I was watching a movie while my sisters were in the computer room doing homework. My mom got a phone call from my dad and she immediately went into her room. I could hear her yelling and crying. I remember asking my sisters what was happening, but I was left with my questions unanswered. My mom did not come out of her room until the next morning. This left me very confused. When my dad returned home, I watched him pack his bags and leave. He told me he was going to stay at my grandmother's house for a little. I remember watching him leave and as he shut the front door, I stood in front of it and cried. Although neither of my parents explicitly told me that they were getting separated, I knew that my dad leaving meant just that.

This was the beginning of my anxiety. I remember feeling anxious all the time and worried. I did not know what it meant to have "anxiety" at such a young age. When I entered my teens, I went to counselling to determine where my anxiety rooted from and I realized that the first moment I felt it was when my dad left our house. At the time, it was not very common for parents to get divorced. I was unsure what it meant for me and my family. Was I going to lose a relationship with my dad and his side of the family? Would this impact my relationship with my sisters?

Luckily for me, I kept a close relationship with both my parents. I lived with my mom and my sisters, but I would often spend time with my dad. I did not pick sides between my mom and my dad but I was left confused and angry at both of my parents. I couldn't understand why this was happening and I felt like my family left me in the dark because I was so young.

My mom and father separated in the month of February 2003. I do not remember how it impacted me in school because in March 2003, my father was diagnosed with Lymphoma. Many of my childhood memories, including those at school, I have blocked out due to my anger, confusion, sadness and anxiety. No matter how hard I try to remember, there are still so many questions I have. I continue to ask my family about my childhood such as "why did dad and mom separate" because these are moments that I refuse to remember. At the time of my mom and dad's separation, I felt like my family was falling apart and it could not get any worse. How was I going to have a mom and a dad who lived in two separate houses? However, the worst was yet to come.

A year after my father's diagnosis, he died. When my father was diagnosed with cancer, my mom and dad got back together. I remember my mom never leaving his side. My mom and dad showed so much affection to one another when I was growing up and this affection returned when my father was ill. Although I was sad about my father's illness, I was almost grateful that they were back together because of it. Being so young, I was in denial that this illness would cause me to lose my father, so I tended to look on the bright side of things before they took a turn for the worst. Once my father got sick, I blocked out the fact that my parents ever separated.

Childhood Loss and Grief

    When discussing my childhood, I barely ever think or refer to the time that my parents separated. As an adult this has impacted me in many ways. I continue to suffer from anxiety of my past which affects many decisions and moments that I experience in today's day and age. It has also impacted me in the sense that I fear change due to the fact that in those two years, my life had changed forever. It not only changed my life for the 10-year-old little girl that I once was when it occurred, but it continues to change my life today and forever. No matter my age or where I am at in life. Although my anxiety streamed from that moment, that is not what defines me as a person. I think about the times that my mother and father shared together, the love they expressed towards each other and my sisters and how, when things got rough, they never left each other's side.

CHAPTER 6

The Parentified Child

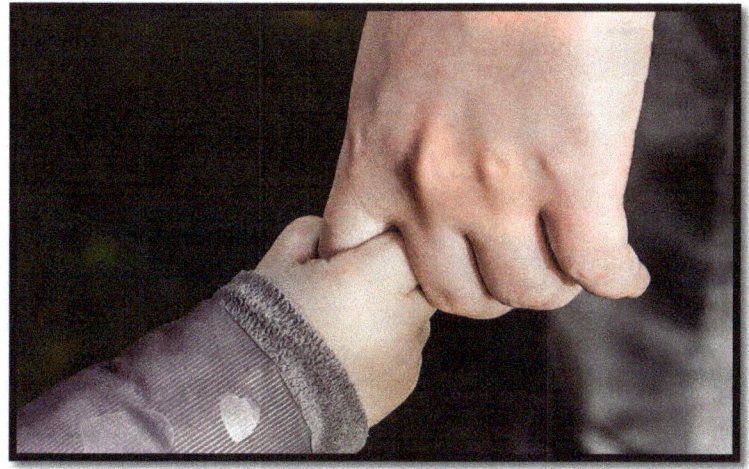

Source: Creative Commons

"Children are not things to be molded, but people to be unfolded."
-Jess Lair

PARENTIFICATION

The term *parentification* was first utilized by Boszormenyi-Nagy and Spark (1973) to describe relationships where parental characteristics are projected onto the child. The process of parentification is often seen when the child performs chores or offers emotional support for the parent; however, parent-child roles frequently become less defined on a temporary basis during times of stress and crisis in the family. Family dynamics such as divorce and the death of a parent can sometimes overburden children with the responsibility of protecting their parents, siblings, and the family as a whole. In circumstances, such as these, *parentified children* or *parentification* entails a functional and/or emotional role reversal where children sacrifice their own needs for attention, comfort, and guidance in order to care for the emotional and physical needs of their parents. The parentified child believes that his/her parent is vulnerable and in need of protection, so he/she will sacrifice himself/herself in order to spare the parent hurt feelings that may destroy the parent and leave the child abandoned (Engelhardt, 2012; Earley & Cushway, 2002; Chase, 1999; James, 1989).

Generational divisions and boundaries exist in families in order to protect spousal bonds and to ensure developmentally appropriate individuation of children from their parents. Minuchin (1967) studied the boundaries that exist in families in terms of systems. Minuchin (1967) treated parentification as the crossing of boundaries between subsystems; children enter the parent subsystem, simultaneously losing their place in the subsystem of childhood. Blurred boundaries in the family system leaves children with too many adult responsibilities, which impacts child development (Ostrowki, Sikorska, & Gerc, 2015).

According to the system theory perspective, parentification helps to maintain balance within the family when boundaries are altered during times of stress such as divorce or the death of a parent. Parentification in these circumstances may manifest for children in two forms: child-as-parent, or child-as-mate (Engelhardt, 2012; Earley & Cushway, 2002; Chase, 1999; James, 1989).

Parentification in Childhood

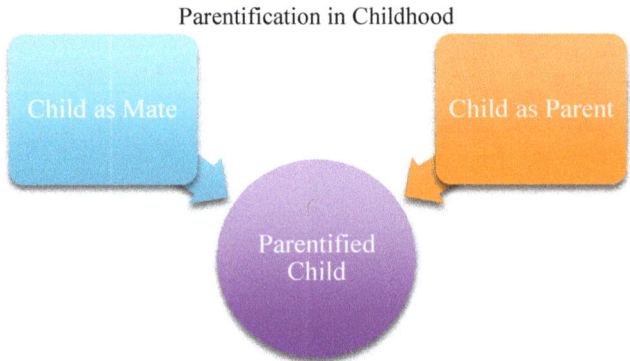

Source: Merenda

As depicted in the above figure, parentification in childhood is also known as *role reversal*. This describes a child acting as a parent to their parent, or a child acting as a

Chapter Six: The Parentified Child

partner to their parent. *Child-as-parent* role reversal includes defending the parent or acting as a parent to siblings. *Child-as-mate* role reversal represents when the child acts as confident, friend or decision-maker for the parent (Engelhardt, 2012; Earley & Cushway, 2002; Chase, 1999; James, 1989).

Child-as-mate role reversal is also known as ***spousification.*** The child replaces the physically or emotionally absent parent by providing the remaining parent with support and caring for their needs (Ostrowki, Sikorska, & Gerc, 2015).

- Logistical parenting tasks (preparing meals, caring for younger siblings, household chores)
- Emotional parenting tasks (providing for or responding to the emotional needs of the family)

Source: Merenda

Parentification can be considered by some as a form of child neglect as it interrupts development through the denial of children's basic necessities and experiences. In a parentification relationship, the parent is unable or unwilling to uphold his/her responsibility to physically and emotionally care for his/her child. Therefore, the child provides the physical and emotional support that he/she would normally receive from the parent, that way, the child can develop closeness with the parent and avoid feelings of loss, anxiety, and rejection. The child interprets these responsibilities as necessary and more important than his/her own needs. As a result, the parentified child misses out on developmentally appropriate activities such as the formation of healthy interpersonal relationships, the development of secure attachment to caregivers, and the differentiation of self, all of which are necessary and a part of typical childhood experiences (Engelhardt, 2012; Earley & Cushway, 2002; Chase, 1999; James, 1989). Child psychologist Elkind (1981) described this as the ***hurried child.***

INSTRUMENTAL AND EMOTIONAL PARENTIFICATION

There are two subtypes of parentification, each of which may be associated with different consequences for child development. ***Instrumental parentification*** is commonly observed in family systems where one or both parents require daily care or are unable to fulfill logistical responsibilities due to illness or other factors. Instrumental parentification is considered to have less of a negative impact on child development because it can foster a sense of accomplishment and competence for the child, if regular parental support and acknowledgment is available and provided. ***Emotional parentification*** is commonly observed in family systems where a parent suffers from mental illness or adult attachment issues and it is considered more

Childhood Loss and Grief

destructive for child development than instrumental parentification (Engelhardt, 2012; Earley & Cushway, 2002; Chase, 1999; James, 1989).

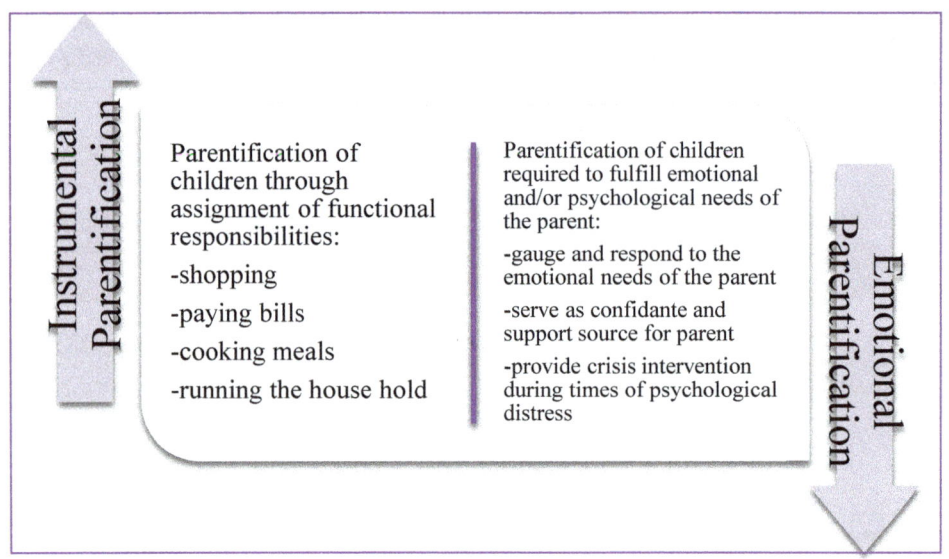

Source: Merenda

OUTCOMES OF PARENTIFICATION

Responding to parental need is not completely problematic because it can help the child develop sensitivities and reciprocity with others. As a result of enacting a parental role, children may learn to be responsible and giving, which can lead to healthy identity formation and self-esteem. In addition, children gain trustworthiness and are able to be caring and affectionate (Engelhardt, 2012; Earley & Cushway, 2002; Chase, 1999; James, 1989).

However, in extreme cases when parent's dependency is too great and when the parent stops structuring and protecting the child from taking on too much responsibility, the parentified child may learn that his/her needs are less important and they may become depleted of energy and time for their school work, friendships, and childhood activities. Furthermore, when adults relinquish parental responsibility, children relinquish their childhood and the range of developmental needs, pleasures, struggles, and opportunities that come with childhood (Engelhardt, 2012; Earley & Cushway, 2002; Chase, 1999; James, 1989).

Outcomes of Parentification in Childhood

- Depression and anxiety
- Somatic symptoms such as headaches and stomachaches
- Aggression and disruptive behaviours
- Social difficulties, lower competency in interpersonal relationships
- Excessive guilt
- Academic problems, high absenteeism and poor grades
- Limited participation in play activities and when they do play, they need to be given specific instruction on how to play

Source: Merenda

Parentification and Defense Mechanisms

When children take on the responsibility of caring for a parent, they are not capable of fully caring for themselves. They lack security, hope, confidence and trust in their world. Children living in this state on chronic anxiety, tension and uncertainty are forced to use various defense mechanisms Ostrowki, Sikorska, & Gerc, 2015.

The defense mechanism most closely related to parentification is dissociation. **Dissociation** refers to autobiographical memory disturbances (verbal), but not procedural memory (non-verbal). In this case, children don't remember traumatic experiences that cause painful feelings, but these traumatic experiences can cause disease symptoms. Mental suffering is replaced with physical suffering because that is easier for children to handle. By doing so, the positive image of the parent is preserved, and any anger or resentment towards the parent is hidden in the unconscious. This allows children to maintain the role of someone who sacrifices their own good for the good of their parent (Ostrowki, Sikorska, & Gerc, 2015).

CHAPTER 7

How Life-Threatening Illnesses Affect Children

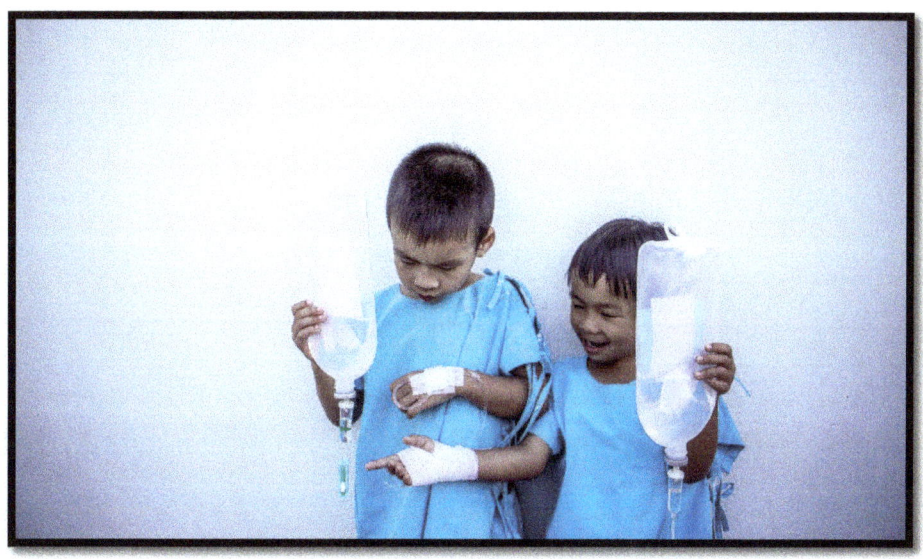

Source: Creative Commons

"Sometimes superheroes reside in the hearts of small children fighting big battles."
-Anonymous

A life-threatening illness is any illness that engenders life and has a significant risk of death (Doka, 1993). Doka (1993) states that the experience of life-threatening illness can be viewed as a series of phases.

Phases of a Life-Threatening Illness

Pre-Diagnosis Phase
- Prior to diagnosis
- Child may complain of various physical symptoms

Diagnostic Phase
- Illness is named
- Parents are coping with the crisis of possible death

Chronic Phase
- Medical and hospital visits; therapies; medication.
- Physical changes
- Adaptation to the loss of familiar events and relationships

Terminal Phase
- Death is inevitable
- Emphasis on providing pain-free treatment

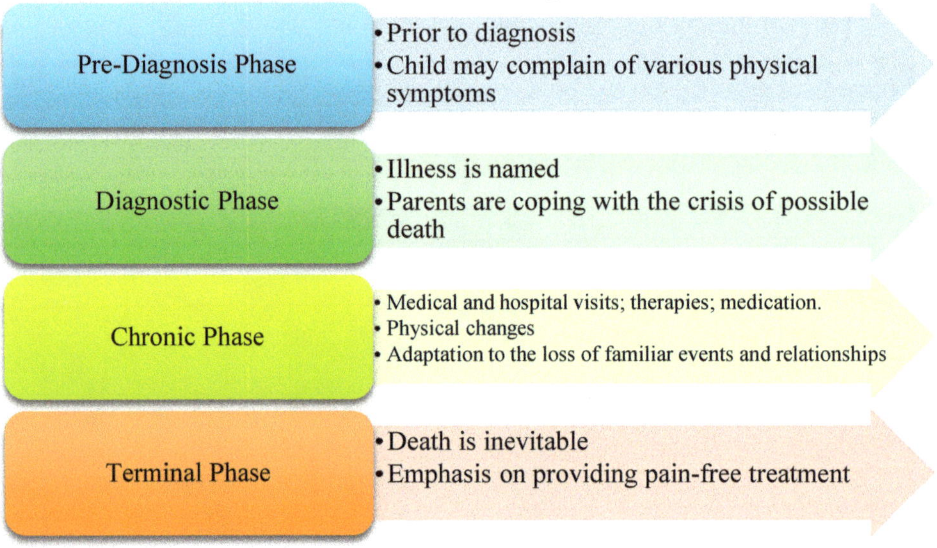

Source: Merenda

The above figure shows how life-threatening illnesses affect children in a variety of ways. Their playful and carefree world is suddenly shaken by the threat of the unknown, medical protocols, multiple health professionals, painful procedures, schedule changes, and overall uncertainty.

Life as they know it is shattered by a loss of control in how the illness affects his or her body and mind, but also in how it affects the child's secure world of family, friends, and routine.

Doka (1993) also suggests the following task-based model for understanding the individual process of addressing life-threatening illness.

In general, the four tasks are: "(1) Respond to the physical fact of disease; (2) Take steps to cope with the reality of the disease; (3) Preserve self-concept and relationships with others in the face of disease; (4) Dealing with effective and existential spiritual issues created or reactivated by the disease" (as cited in Doka, 1995, p. 45).

Children will cope with the tasks just as adults will; however, there are special concerns when children are coping with terminal illnesses. Children are often protected by not being told that they are ill or denied the opportunity to speak about their illness or their fears of death. Sometimes, parents or caregivers will provide children with the name of the illness, but reserve facts or limit discussion of the prognosis (Doka, 1995).

General	Acute Phase	Chronic Phase	Terminal Phase
1. Responding to the physical fact of disease	1. Understanding the disease	1. Managing symptoms and side effects	1. Dealing with symptoms, discomfort, pain, and incapacitation
2. Taking steps to cope with the reality of disease	2. Maximizing health and lifestyle	2. Carrying out health regime	2. Managing health procedures and institutional stress
	3. Maximizing one's coping strengths and limiting weakness	3. Preventing and managing health crisis	3. Managing stress and examining coping
	4. Developing strategies to deal with the issues created by the disease	4. Managing stress and examining coping	4. Dealing effectively with caregivers
		5. Maximizing social support and minimizing isolation	5. Preparing for death and saying goodbye
		6. Normalizing life in the face of the disease	
		7. Dealing with financial concerns	
3. Preserving self-concept and relationships with others in the face of disease	5. Exploring the effects of the diagnosis on a sense of self and others	8. Preserving self-concept	6. Preserving self-concept
		9. Redefining relationships with others throughout the course of the disease	7. Preserving appropriate relationships with family and friends
4. Dealing with affective and existential/spiritual issues created or reactivated by the disease	6. Ventilating feelings and fears	10. Ventilating feelings and fears	8. Ventilating feelings and fears
	7. Incorporating present reality of diagnosis into one's sense of past and future	11. Finding meaning in suffering, chronicity, uncertainty, and decline	9. Finding meaning in life and death

Source: Merenda

CHILDREN'S RIGHT TO INFORMATION AND DECISION MAKING POWER

In multiple countries, all around the world, children have the right to be given truthful and accurate information about their condition. Since 1989, the United Nations Convention on the Rights of the Child has been considered an important declaration of full human rights for every child (Martenson & Fagerskiold, 2007). The Convention clearly states every child has the right to self-determination, dignity, respect, non-interference, and the right to make informed decisions (Coyne, 2008). In 2002, the United Nations held the UN General Assembly on Children, where the nations of the world dedicated themselves to improving the circumstance of children and young individuals (UN General Assembly on Children, 2002). The UN General Assembly on Children led to the creation of a document called, "A World Fit for Children." Quoting from it, the UN General Assembly on Children (2002) states that, "Children, including adolescents, must be enabled to exercise their right to express their views freely, according to their evolving capacity, and build self-esteem, acquire knowledge and skills, such as those for conflict resolution, decision-making and communication, to meet the challenges of life...must be respected and promoted and their views taken into account in all matters affecting them, the views of the child being given due weights in accordance with the age and maturity of the child." (A World Fit for Children, p. 7).

The Canadian Pediatric Society states that children should have a right to express themselves. Decisions involving children should be made in collaboration with the children, their parents, and healthcare professionals. The Canadian Pediatric Society also states that once children have the competence to make decisions, fully understand their illness, understand the main purpose of interventions, and comprehend the consequences of consent or dissent and the extent of what could occur children should then be the primary decision-makers (Rogers, et al., 2009).

Although the United Nations Convention on the Rights of the Child and the Canadian Pediatric Society encourage children as significant participants in decision-making about matters affecting them, there appears to be an unequal power relationship between children, parents, and healthcare professionals which limits children's participation in their personal healthcare (Bricher, 2000). Despite children's right to express their views and participate in making informed decisions about matters affecting themselves, parents and caregivers commonly refrain from communicating information to children about their illness. Adults try to protect children, fearing if they know too much about their own illness, it may depress or dishearten them (Corr & Corr, 1996).

Terminally ill children are viewed as potentially vulnerable and consequently, they are more at risk of having their views ignored or dishonoured by adults who are considered more competent to make healthcare decisions on children's behalf (Coyne, 2006).

Nevertheless, research has demonstrated that attempts to protect children from illness and death are ineffective for the following reasons (Bluebond-Langner, 1978; Doka, 1982). First, children can acquire a degree of medical sophistication in multiple ways. In middle childhood, they study diseases, they may have had experiences with the illnesses of others, and have obtained information about disease from the media.

Second, children have external cues concerning their own health situation. They can sense the anxieties and concerns radiating from the adults around them. They recognize when conversations cease when they enter the room, and they witness friends and relatives visiting from distant places. Third, children respond to their own internal cues. They know that they are in pain, they can sense when they are weaker and more sick. Studies have indicated that children with life-threatening illnesses were well aware of their condition even when adults withdrew information from them (Corr & Corr, 1996).

CHILDREN'S COMPETENCY TO PARTICIPATE IN MEDICAL DECISIONS

Competence means having "...the ability to perform a task" (Martenson & Fagerskiold, 2007, p. 3132). Decision-making competence means having the capacity to make a decision. In order to make a decision, one must be competent enough to do so (Martenson & Fagerskiold, 2007). Children's decision-making competency in their personal healthcare is a controversial topic. Parents typically make decisions on children's behalf because parents are assumed to know what is in their children's best interest. However, determining what is in children's best interest is subject to opposing values among children, parents, and healthcare professionals. In order to find out what is in children's best interest, they should be encouraged to express their opinion in matters regarding themselves and children should be encouraged to participate in personal medical decisions (Runeson, Eriskar, Elander, & Hermeren, 2001).

Children's level of cognitive development influences their views. According to Piaget's cognitive development theory children progress from sensorimotor awareness in infancy, to fantasized interpretation of reality in the preschool years, to concrete and logical thinking in the school-age years, and finally, to abstract thinking in adolescence. Children's level of development mediates what they are thinking about or concerned about (Rogers et al., 2009).

Children's interpretation of their bodies, of illness causation, illness treatment, life, and death progresses through this cognitive path (Rogers et al., 2009). According to Harrison et al. (1997), most children belong to one of these three groups with respect to their developmental stage and the level of involvement in their personal healthcare that is encouraged by parents and healthcare professionals.

As children grow and progress through the stages of development, they develop decision-making skills, the ability to reason, an understanding of death and the ability to imagine a future for themselves. Although developmental stages depict a general sense of capacities, two children of the same age will not necessarily have the same ability or inability to make decisions. As a result, a child's age should not determine his or her level of competency. Furthermore, children with a chronic or terminal illness may have experiences that bestow them with insight and maturity beyond their developmental stage. Allowing even young children to make decisions about simple matters surrounding their health and treatment facilitates the development of skills that they will need in order to make complex decisions throughout the course of their lives (Harrison et al., 1997).

Childhood Loss and Grief

Children from Noyes (2000), study expressed their wish for consultation and information to understand their diagnosis, participate in their personal care, and prepare themselves for procedures. When children acquire knowledge about their diagnosis and are more involved in their care, they are more willing to cooperate with treatment, appear less upset, and recover better. When children are encouraged to participate in their healthcare they feel a renewed sense of control and independence because they understand their diagnosis and children feel competent enough to be a part of the decision-making process (Coyne, 2006).

Common Effects of Illness and Chronic Pain on Child Development

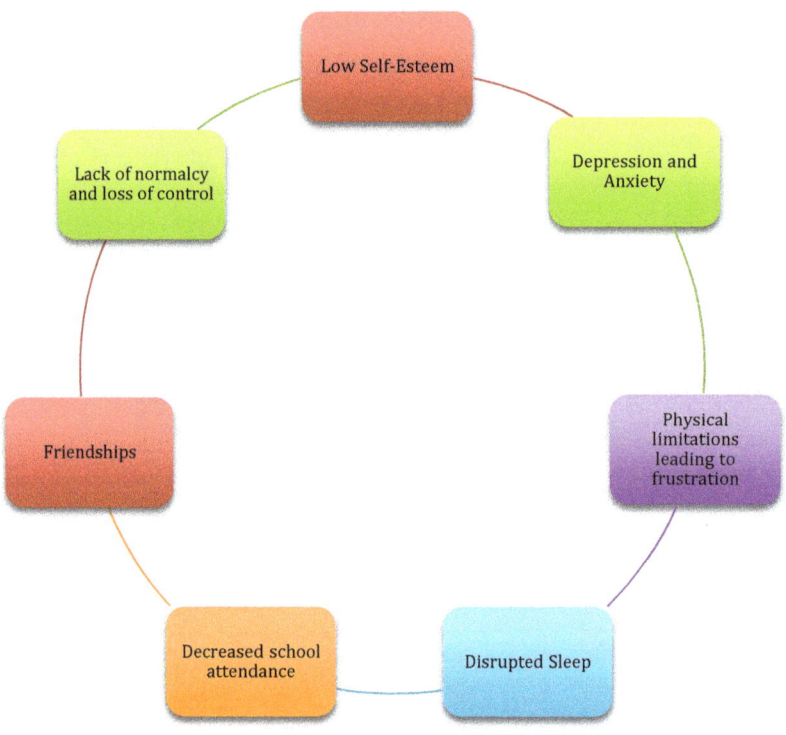

Source: Merenda

Desire for Information and Control

Many studies conducted with children in hospitals report that children want parents and healthcare professionals to respect their autonomy. Children want to be consulted and involved in general decisions about their healthcare and treatment. Many children spoke about needing information from their parents and healthcare professionals in order to understand their illness and treatment plan, be involved in their own healthcare, prepare themselves for procedures, and develop coping mechanisms that will assist them in getting well again.

Children commonly use several strategies to obtain information, such as asking parents and healthcare professionals questions; observing and talking to other children on the same unit with the same illness; getting books from the local library; and comparing experiences with medical television programs and with past experiences visiting relatives in the hospital. Children use these strategies to seek information because information seeking is a predominant coping strategy used by children during hospitalization (Coyne, 2006). Seeking information independently may be more harmful than good for children. Children might misinterpret information and develop unnecessary and incorrect conclusions. Misinterpreting information can create a lot more anxiety for children because they may believe their diagnosis and medical circumstances are more negative than they really are. Providing children with information about their diagnosis prevents them from seeking information on their own.

Children want to be involved in discussions about their care. They commonly report feeling upset, angry, and depressed when parents and healthcare professionals do not involve them or when parents and healthcare professionals give children false information (Coyne, 2006). Parents and healthcare professionals generally shield children from hearing negative information because they want to block children's knowledge from the complicated realities of life and death. Parents are frightened to give children information; as a result, parents tell children mistruths or partial truths about the children's illness. Parents also frequently avoid discussing the possibility of death with terminally ill children. In many cases, children intuitively know when something is wrong with their body and health; therefore, mistruths, partial truths, and diminishing the truth cause greater fear and anxiety for children. Children have the capacity to understand what is happening to their body and they deserve to be told the truth about their health condition. Receiving information and being informed of the seriousness of the illness can be reassuring for children (Rogers et al., 2009). Children have a need for information and support to participate in decisions (Coad & Shaw, 2008).

HOSPITALIZATION

Illness causes disruption to children's sense of well-being and hospitalization may represent a threat to children's independence, typical self-caring abilities, and self-control. A potentially stressful and of particular significance for hospitalized children is concern about loss of control and feelings of dependence (Coyne, 2006). Children typically want to be involved in their own care and decision-making so that they can exercise some control over what is happening to their body as well as exert control over the unfamiliar environment. As a result, children should always have the right to express their opinion, whether they are considered competent or not. This is necessary for children to become competent decision-makers in their personal healthcare. Children's autonomy in decision-making is important because it assists them to understand their health condition and it gives them a voice, which enables them to ask questions and express their opinions (Rogers et al., 2009).

Stressors of Hospitalization

Hospitalization creates a series of traumatic and stressful events that produce uncertainty for children. Bricher (2002) states, "Children admitted to the hospital are vulnerable because of their illness, their limitation of understanding, and because they have so little control over what is happening to them" (p. 100). Besides the physiological effects of the health problem, the impact of illness and hospitalization on a child includes anxiety and fear related to the process of hospitalization and the possibility of bodily pain from tests and procedures (Kyle, 2008).

Additionally, children are separated from their homes, families, friends, and everything that is familiar to them. This often results in *separation anxiety,* which can be defined as distress related to removal from family and familiar surroundings. There is a feeling of loss of control over their lives and sometimes their emotions and behaviour. This results in anger, guilt, acting out, and sometimes regression (Kyle, 2008).

Children who are hospitalized experience a significant loss of control, increasing the perception of threat, affecting their coping skills. Children lose control over routine self-care, their usual tasks and play routine, as well as decisions related to the care of their own bodies. Children's usual routine is disrupted; they cannot choose what to do and at what time (Kyle, 2008).

Hospitalization also affects a child's control over decisions related to his/her body. Treatments and procedures are often invasive and children do not have the option to refuse to undergo them.

Phase 1: Protest
- Child is separated from parents/caretaker
- Lasts for a few hours-several days
- Great distress; crying, expressing agitation, rejects others who attemtp to comfort
- Inconsolable grief

Phase 2: Dispair
- Exhibited if the parent does not return within a short time
- Displays hopelessness by withdrawing from others, becoming quiet without crying, apathic, depressed, distinerest in play and food.

Phase 3: Detachment
- Child forms coping mechanisms to protect himslef/herself from further emotional paid
- Shows interest in the environment, starts to play again, and forms superficial relationships with people in the environment

Source: Merenda

Separation Anxiety

Separation anxiety is a major stressor for children of certain ages. It occurs more commonly in children from middle infancy throughout the preschool years. Separation anxiety consists of three stages during which children exhibit certain behaviours to the stress of the separation (Kyle, 2008).

REACTION TO HOSPITALIZATION

Children's responses to the stressors of fear, separation anxiety, and loss of control vary depending on their age and developmental level.

Infants and Toddlers

Infants and toddlers are rapidly growing, developing, and establishing a healthy attachment to their parents/primary caregivers. They are dependent on others for nurture and protection and they gain a sense of trust in the world through reciprocal relationships. Infants and toddlers require a secure pattern of restful sleep, satisfaction of basic needs, relaxation of body systems, and spontaneous response to communication and gentle stimuli (Nagera, 1978; Kyle, 2008). As a result, separation anxiety, due to separation from the child's family, particularly the mother, is the major stressor during hospitalization for these two age groups (Nagera, 1978).

Stages of Separation Anxiety for Infants and Toddlers

- **Protest:** Protest loudly, watch for their mother, and cry continuously until they fall asleep.

- **Despair:** Anger turns to despair. Children look sad and lonely, they may refuse to eat, they become depressed and move less.

- **Denial:** Children deny the need for their mother by appearing detached and uninterested in her visits. Prolonged deprivation of a maternal presence can lead to: delayed biological maturation and irreversible damage to the cognitive and intellectual functioning of the child.

Toddlers are more aware of self and can communicate their needs. Toddlers need opportunities to explore and they need consistent routines. When toddlers are hospitalized, the development of their autonomy is disrupted (Nagera, 1978; Kyle, 2008).

As a result, toddlers react to the loss of control their experience while in the hospital. Activity limits, decreased opportunities for choices, and interrupted rituals lead to feelings of powerlessness. It is common for toddlers to respond to feelings of powerlessness with regression. They abandon acquired skills and demand assistance with tasks that they were previously able to complete independently (Nagera, 1978; Kyle, 2008).

Preschoolers

The preschool child has better verbal and developmental skills to adapt to various situations. However, hospitalization can still be a stressful experience leading to regression in behaviour, physical capabilities, and language development (Nagera, 1978; Kyle, 2008).

Preschoolers may understand that they are in the hospital, but they may not understand their illness or the cause of the illness. Preschoolers fear mutilation and are afraid of intrusive procedures (Nagera, 1978; Kyle, 2008). Preschooler's thinking is egocentric; they have difficulty distinguishing between fantasy and reality. They believe they are powerful and control the world around them; therefore, they believe that a personal action or thought caused their illness, leading to guilt and shame (Nagera, 1978; Kyle, 2008).

Although not as obviously as the infant and toddler, preschoolers also experience separation anxiety. They may act uncooperatively and frequently ask for their parents. Preschoolers are also significantly affected by loss of control because their schedules have changed and they are physically restricted (Nagera, 1978; Kyle, 2008).

One of the major ways preschoolers cope with their environment is through fantasizing. This fantasizing often leads to fear. As a result, hospitalized preschoolers often have nightmares and are afraid of unfamiliar sounds and sights. *Animism,* a belief that inanimate objects have life, is a common concern for preschoolers.

Therefore, preschoolers often fear hospital machinery and equipment because they believe it is alive and will harm them. This causes feelings of powerlessness (Nagera, 1978; Kyle, 2008).

School-Aged Children

School-age children may show some signs of parental and peer separation anxiety when they are ill and hospitalized. They may fear that their peers will forget them while they are away from school. School-age children also fear pain and permanent disability or body disfigurement. School-age children may also fear death (Nagera, 1978; Kyle, 2008).

School-age children are developing confidence in controlling their feelings and actions. Hospitalization causes them to feel out of control because it interrupts their routine and limits their independence. They may exhibit resistive behaviours and have changes in signs in response to stress. Anger, boredom, frustration, and disinterest are all common indicators of loss of control (Nagera, 1978; Kyle, 2008).

Childhood Loss and Grief

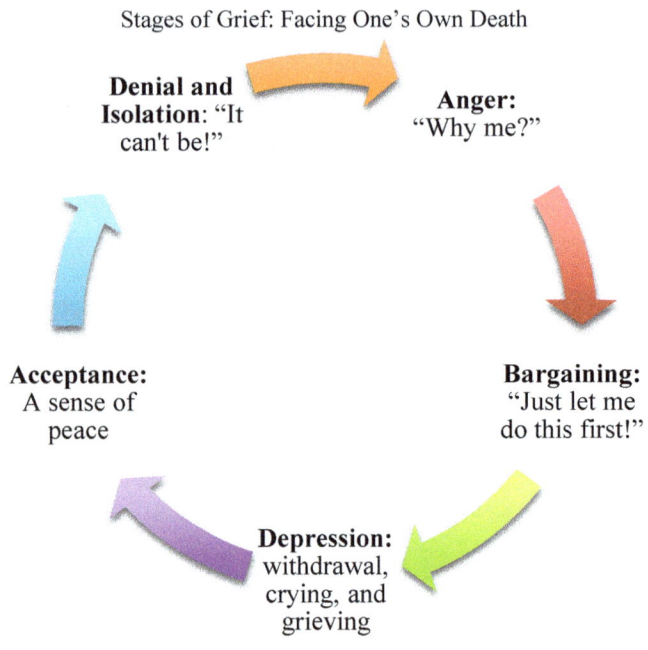

Source: Merenda

School attendance is important for academic and social skill development. However, when school-age children are ill and frequently hospitalized, school engagement is affected, as is the achievement of important educational milestones and skill acquisition.

Academic Difficulties

The most prominent impact of illness and hospitalization for school-age children is academic difficulties including: minimal education accommodations, difficulty meeting curriculum requirements; continuously trying to play "catch up", causing anxiety; impaired academic functioning due to drowsiness, fatigue, nausea, increased irritability, decreased attention span, impaired learning (Duggan, Medway, & Bunke, 2004).

Chapter Seven: How Life-Threatening Illnesses Affect Children

Impact of Illness on Education

[Diagram: A funnel containing three circles labeled "Behavioural Problems", "School Absenteeism", and "Academic Difficulties", flowing down to:]

Student Performance

Source: Merenda

Behavioural Problems

School-aged children who are ill and are hospitalized for lengthy periods of time often develop *school phobia.* School phobia occurs when children have prolonged absences from school, with little peer interaction, leading to discomfort and fear (Duggan, Medway, & Bunke, 2004)

School Absenteeism

School attendance is critical for social competence. School provides opportunities for children to learn; socialize with their peers; experience success; and develop increased independence and control over their environment. School is a safe place for children because it is the only place where they are viewed as children rather than patients (Duggan, Medway, & Bunke, 2004). Inability to attend school due to illness and/or hospitalization can lead to decreased self-esteem and hopelessness about the future (Duggan, Medway, & Bunke, 2004)

Characteristics of School Phobia

- Difficulty adjusting to the social demands of school
- Fear that peers may shun them because they are concerned that the disease is contagious
- Fear of being judged based on physical appearance (hair loss, amputations, ambulatory devices such as wheelchairs and walkers

Source: Merenda

COMMON REACTIONS FROM FAMILY

Family systems theory is a school of thought which holds that a family is a social system, a living organism, in which the members operate in a dynamic, reciprocal relationship. This relationship makes the whole (family) greater than the individual parts (each family member). Applied to childhood illness and hospitalization, family systems theory tells us that the whole family is affected (Price & Gwin, 2008; Webb, 2009).

The way in which childhood illness and hospitalization impacts families depends on family dynamics (e.g. single parents versus two parent households), the type of illness, the child's developmental age, social class, marital harmony, culture, and ethnicity. Pressures such as financial or time burdens, worries about the future, treatment regimen, loss of privacy, and the responsibility of making medical decisions are some of the factors that affect families (Price & Gwin, 2008; Webb, 2009).

For families, childhood illness is a crisis. It interrupts the dynamic balance by which family members operate, causing a sense of disorganization and upheaval. Family members often feel disconnected and roles are transformed. What once was "normal" gives way, and a new "normal" must be developed (Price & Gwin, 2008; Webb, 2009).

Upon diagnosis, parents may initially feel guilt, helpless, and anxious. They often blame themselves for the child's illness. Parents may also fear the unknown because they are unfamiliar with the hospital settings, procedures, treatments, and the disease itself (Price & Gwin, 2008; Webb, 2009).

According to Patterson & Garwick (1994), the reaction of parents is threefold (as cited in Webb, 2009):

Chapter Seven: How Life-Threatening Illnesses Affect Chidren

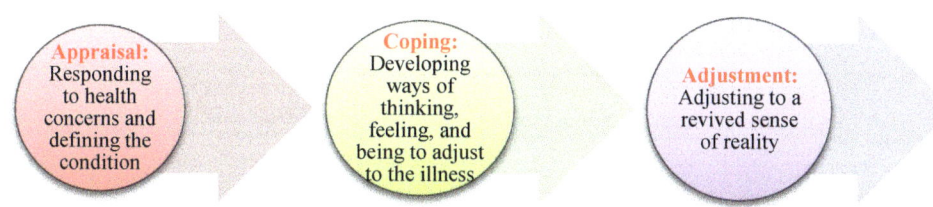

Source: Merenda

Similarly, Clarke-Steffen (1993) developed a four-stage model depicting how families adjust to a child's illness, as depicted in the figure below (as cited in Webb, 2009).

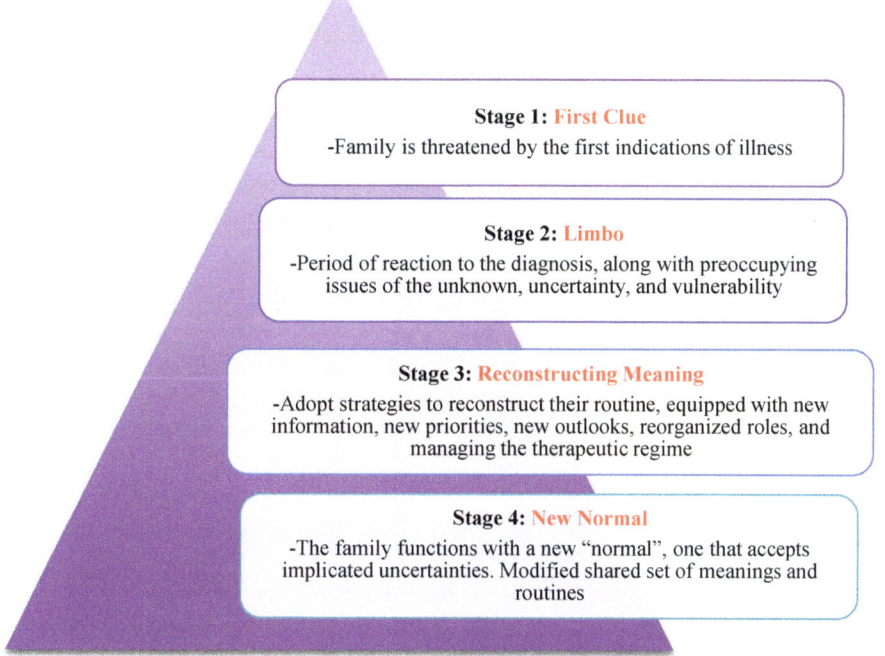

Source: Merenda

Siblings are also affected when a child is hospitalized. As described in the subsequent figure, sibling of children who have a life-threatening illness may experience anger, resentment, jealousy, and guilt. Suddenly attention is focused on the sick child and siblings may feel neglected. When routines are changed and family members are separated, the needs of the siblings may not be met. Parents are unlikely their usual selves, as they are anxious and their priorities have changed (Tindall, 1999).

Child's Reaction to a Sibling's Life-Threatening Disease

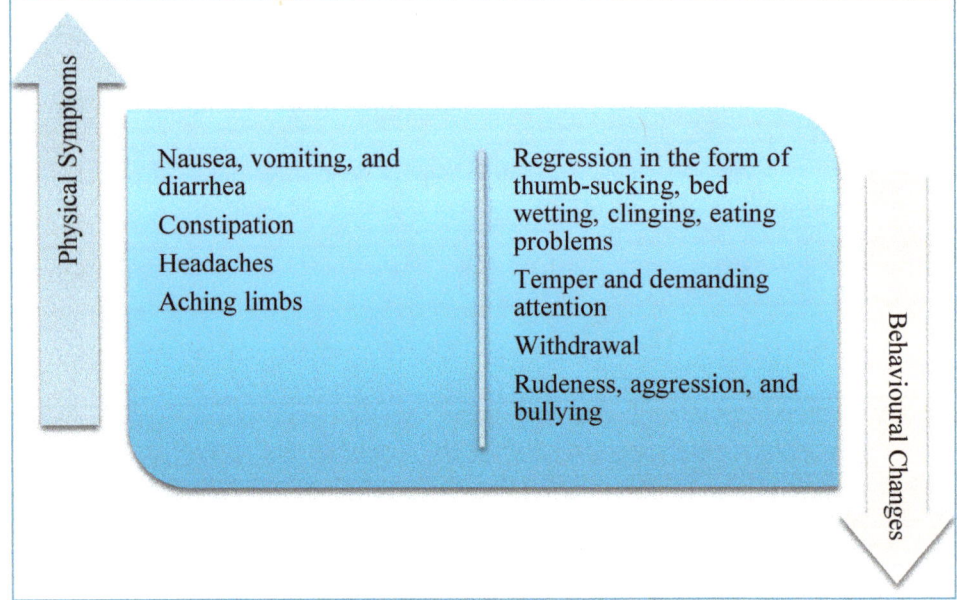

Source: Merenda

Chapter Seven: How Life-Threatening Illnesses Affect Chidren

CASE STUDIES

Maxwell (Written by Dr. Nikki Martyn)

Developmental History

Maxwell was conceived by Caucasian parents in their 40's. Mom was pregnant with his sister when he was 12 months old, he was diagnosed and treated for cancer at 18 months old. Mom is a family physician and dad employed by a bank, they are considered to be within the upper middle socio-economic status. They reside in a major city in Canada. They employed nannies to care for the children for most of his early life until he began at the treatment school at 2.5 years.

Mom reports a normal labour and delivery, her son Maxwell arrived 8 days post term via a vaginal delivery. He was in the occipitoposterior position and required vacuum assistance. His birth weight was 8 lbs 5 ounces. There were no complications during the pregnancy apart from some nausea, which necessitated the use of Diclectin during the first trimester. Ultrasounds were normal and at delivery there was no need for resuscitation. There were no complications during the post-natal period and no history of jaundice or seizures. He was discharged from the hospital at 2 days. He was breastfed for 7.5 months and then bottle-fed. He was home with his mother until 7 months of age. He was then cared for by a Filipino nanny from 7 months to 11 months of age. A new Filipino nanny started at 11 months and was the primary caregiver until she left around 2.5 years old.

Maxwell was described by his mother as a "difficult baby" and was quite colicky during the first few months of his life. He would cry a lot, this settled by 6 months of age. His mother recalls that he would be content in his jolly jumper for at least an hour at a time. As an infant, his mom recalls he would be content on his own, he would stay in his crib with his toys for quite some time. At 15 months, he would say "mama" and "dada" but did not always use the words appropriately. He then reportedly stopped using those words and did not start again until after his surgery at 21 months. He was diagnosed with Wilms disease at 19 months old and received invasive treatment. He physically recovered well.

Medical History

He was developing well until July 2007 when he had 3 episodes of unexplained fevers. His mother noted an abdominal mass and he was diagnosed with Wilms tumor at 19 months of age at an Internationally renowned children's hospital. He was hospitalized for two weeks. The tumor and his right kidney were removed. There was no spread of the tumor. He received chemotherapy. He has had a successful recovery.

Following the surgery and chemotherapy at 2.5 years, his parents noticed he was not developing as other children and was displaying verbal regression. His family physician referred him to a Child Developmental Clinic at a local hospital in a major city in Canada. The reason for the referral was "speech and language delay, decreased eye contact, decreased social interactions." A developmental paediatrician and occupational therapist at the Internationally renowned children's hospital conducted an assessment in which a diagnosis of severe autism was provided.

During the assessment, they noted "he demonstrates significant, immediate echolalia." When given a choice, he would often repeat back the choice, he also displayed scripted echolalia from television shows. The assessment commented that "he does not always co-ordinate distal pointing with eye contact." Also, noting he did not demonstrate a consistent response to his name, "if a parent walks into the room and makes comments without getting his attention first, he is not likely to respond. He often does not respond to questions that are asked of him even though he may know the answers." He initiates an interaction and requests by pulling the person to what he wants including in his interaction with children and does not always demonstrate a responsive social smile, indicating that his language and communication was consistent with the diagnosis of autism. This was consistent with the Vineland assessment performed during the same time period, which indicated below average in communication and low skills in socialization, daily living and motor skills domains.

During the assessment, it was observed that he "lined up cars and after arranging and ordering cars and other toys in a specific area on the floor, he would then take the cars and objects one by one and relocate them to another area. This ritualistic and repetitive behavior continued for quite some time." It was noted, "he would often tilt his head and seemed to be watching the wheels up close." "At times the examiner would call his name or his parents might call his name or ask a question, but he would not respond. His selection and interest in toys was limited. Although he demonstrated some functional play with the cars, his play was mostly nonfunctional, putting them in these arrangements. When the examiner went to get a plane for him, he was very excited and showed some upper extremity tensing and flapping. He was mostly quiet during this play but would intermittently label objects as he found them. He would also make sounds and do some sing songy sounds. He also demonstrated some immediate echolalia to words that were said in the adult discussion. He did not demonstrate any difficult behavior except when his organization of cars on the floor was disrupted."

Therapeutic School

The mindwerx4kids model provided an individualized model of group care for children aged between 1 – 6 years of age. The program provided enriching experiences to enhance cognitive development and also had an equal investment to encouraging social and emotional development and developing such capacities such as caring, having positive relationships, and regulating negative behaviour and emotions. A relationship-based curriculum with attentive caregivers providing emotional support was also a critical part of the program. With a small teacher – child ratio (one teacher to four children) for children who have identified delays or other difficulties and who could benefit from this type of care, to allow extra attention to the individual needs of each child.

In order to link each child's needs to an individualized theme and skill-based curriculum, developmental screening of each child was completed and further assessments provided across various developmental areas when necessary on entry into the program. These assessments may be multidisciplinary and test the child in skill-based areas and in other domains of emotional and social development. For children who are identified as having special needs on this preliminary assessment, further, more in-depth assessment was provided. Once this assessment is completed childcare professionals and psychologists select curricular activities that correspond to each child's needs and integrate them into the child's day according to his or her interests and developmental profile.

Intervention

It was apparent to the staff at mindwerx4kids that Maxwell was not autistic. During an interview with the early interventionist and the director of the school they recalled seeing Maxwell and his mom interact for the first time. "It was 5 o'clock and the other kids were outside…somebody had given him a train set because there was a report that he liked trains. And when I walked in he was on the floor pushing the train back and forth and looking at the wheels." "He stood up and was so excited by the wheels that he looked at them and flapped his arms. But then he looked right away at Mom…immediately there was a joint attention, connection, along with the flapping. And then he looked at one of us and seemed to find us strange, so he hadn't recognized that we were there. Found us strange, stopped flapping, looked backed to Mom, waited for her to look at us, saw that we were safe, and then went back to the trains. And then I put two extra trains in front of the ones that he was pulling along on the other side of the track to force him to get back up because he had laid back down to look at the wheels. And then I indicated something about the wheels and immediately he locked his trains to mine. He was able to stand up, and I said, the wheels go round and round, and he engaged with that. And then I said, look outside and look at the wheels on the cars and he did, he went right over to the window and he flapped at the window again. But it was like we were able to engage with him right after he became comfortable with us. There had been the check of the mom, and there were the repetitive and the stereotypy movements and the lying down, but it almost felt like it was too easy to pull him out."…"Then when the Director and I were saying goodbye I remember him not being able to walk down the stairs properly. Mom seemed very concerned, about almost carrying him or whatever she wanted to do. And I remember, he had a train with him or somebody had a train, and I put it on the bannister and he put his hand on the bannister to move down himself. And I thought, oh he is easy, he is going to be able to walk on his own. I remember him looking at her and saying something to her, either "train" or "mommy," or something that indicated more affective relations, and then they left. I remember standing in the stairs with the director and saying, "he is not autistic" and she agreed." "There were lots of signs for autism, it is just that there were so many, if you saw him on paper he filled all the check marks, but then when you actually saw him it was like they were coping mechanisms."

Over the course of the next 4 years, Maxwell worked with a multidisciplinary team, including a speech and language pathologist, occupational therapist, psychologist, psychiatrist, behavioural therapist and extensively with an early interventionist during the early learning program. He received therapies individually while at the centre and the early interventionist worked with the Early Childhood Educators to ensure his "treatment" recommendations were implemented in the classroom thus creating an inclusive classroom experience.

Conclusion

This is an interesting case of a young child who experienced a trauma during the treatment for cancer *and the loss of his caregiver (Nanny)*. During the hospital, developmental assessment in which autism was diagnosed the following observations were recorded. "He found the Elmo and the Dora doll and brought them over to place them in his mother's lap. When the examiner activated the Elmo doll, he was scared and moved toward his mother but did not look at her for assurance. Instead, he seemed to be backing up into her." There is some suggestion that the backing into his mother and the lack of eye contact was the displaying of trauma behaviours. This was easily missed during the assessment in which he met the DSM IV criteria for moderate to severe autism. However, once observed and developmentally assessed in the treatment school with individualized programming it was discovered that he was experiencing trauma reactions and when provided with emotional and social interventions through relational play based multidisciplinary interventions he "lost" his diagnosis of autism at the age of 6 years from the same developmental pediatrician at the internationally renowned children's hospital who initially diagnosed him.

This clinical investigation demonstrates the importance that high quality, multi-disciplinary, early learning environments have in supporting children and families who have experienced trauma. While understanding the child's development and the interventions implemented to aid in the reversal of the Autism diagnosis and treatment of trauma over the four-year period.

Lauren

My name is Lauren. When I was 15, I was diagnosed with Acute Lymphoblastic Leukemia. This type of cancer is one of the most common forms in children. I had a hard time believing that I could have been diagnosed with this illness. It seemed almost surreal that this could now be my life; at this point, I knew I would have to start fighting for my chance to live.

My family was in shock that their 15-year-old child had just been diagnosed with blood cancer. They were able to find support through their professional community as they were both police officers. My parents were incredible and found the strength and courage to support me. At some points, my family was really all I had – my friends did not really understand the severity of cancer and they couldn't always make time to come and visit me, I don't blame them but I did need them more than they knew. There was a struggle for a sense of normalcy in my life. As a teenager, I missed out on many opportunities to experience a *typical* teenage life. I longed to trade my time in the hospital, for time at school, with my friends, and for the chance to experience the ups and downs of adolescence. Instead, I spent my time fighting for my chance to live.

Chapter Seven: How Life-Threatening Illnesses Affect Chidren

To treat Acute Lymphoblastic Leukemia, I had to go through a 30-month intensive treatment that entails a variety of medical procedures to defeat the virus, and disease. There was a steroid medication that they gave me but in my particular situation, this steroid is a specific medication that is primarily responsible for getting rid of the cancer, the chemotherapy is responsible for keeping you in remission. So, it's a completely necessary medication, there's no way that you can avoid it in your treatment. They would start new medication and then take it away, every week it would be different, and this particular medication that I was on, was only present in my protocol for three weeks and it completely ruined the rest of my life. I developed a rare side effect called Avascular necrosis, AVN for short. Essentially, what that means is that this medication cut off the circulation to my joint. It basically restricted blood flow and most of the joints in my body collapsed shortly after that. Since my treatment, I've had 5 total joint replacements, and I will have to have more in the future. Truthfully, the cancer was really hard and that first year was so terrible, but it's been the side effects as a whole that's affected my life the most. The 6 years after that was just constant joint replacements all one at a time. They're pretty invasive surgeries, I've had three hip replacements. My first hip replacement was unsuccessful, so after 6 months I had to go back, and have it done again. I've had two joint replacements on my right side, one on my left, I had my shoulders replaced, and I'll have to have both my knees replaced in the future. I also have AVN in my neck and back, and obviously, you can't have a spine replacement, so I do struggle with pain management till this day. What I was not anticipating through the process was the pain, the loneliness, and frustration I would face over this 30-month long treatment. The pain was one of the most unbearable parts. A big part of my treatment was having chemotherapy injected into my spine which is essentially a spinal tap, those are so painful, I would have those frequently in the beginning once a week.

I partook in a camp up in Muskoka, it's called Camp Ooch for short. It's a camp that's strictly for children or survivors of cancer that are in pediatric care. It's amazing they have a full oncology staff, oncology nurses on staff all summer, so you can literally be up there all summer, sitting on a Muskoka chair on Lake Roscoe getting chemotherapy on the dock. They have wheel chair accessible high ropes courses, it's just such a special place and was such a humbling experience. I met so many people there that were all in different stages of survivorship, some like myself that were recent—I'd been a survivor for a year. Some of them were survivors for 15 years, they were diagnosed at toddlers. That was a really great experience and something that's super special to me, I still stay in touch with a lot of those people. I met a couple friends at Sick Kids there was one person in particular, his name was Reid, he had this rare bone disease. I was 17 when he passed away he was 19. We had kind of a weird relationship, it was almost like my little cancer boyfriend. We did so much together. There was one New Year's Eve, we were both hospitalised for the holidays and him and I sat at this bench and you could see the fireworks from Toronto city hall, he definitely filled that void of missing my friends my age and teenage stuff. We were in the same stage, both in our treatments and the season of life we were in for teenagers. All the same things that were important to you as a teenager, even just our hair, he could relate. Reid will always hold a special place in my heart.

Today, I am 28 years old and I have followed in my family's footsteps; I'm in policing as well. I'm a 911 dispatcher, I probably would have been an officer if I hadn't been sick, but I think dispatching is the next best thing. My police family is a whole other thing for me, and that was such a huge thing for grieving, not just for me, but for my family. The blue bloods thing is very real. The police force is such a family. Those are the people that are protecting your life when you're out on shifts, and there is such a special bond there. When I got sick, Peel Regional Police, which is Brampton/Mississauga, and everybody rallied around my family. Out of all the cancer stuff that has stuck with me since that time, the only issue that's translated into my everyday life and will continue in my everyday life is just the side effects of my joints, and that's a direct reflection of my cancer, that's my biggest challenge. I also got into public speaking about being a cancer survivor. I got contacted by a lot of the charities that I had benefitted from and it's fun for me. I like sharing my story, but I love when people come and share theirs with me.

Although, my life would have been so different without cancer, I am who I am today because of it. I have been through many circumstances that I would not wish upon anyone, I have had to fight for my life and my health. I have had to watch this disease hurt not only me, but my family. But through it all, I have had to remain me. I have become a person I am proud and happy to be, and I wouldn't change that for the world.

CHAPTER 8

Responding to Grieving Children in the Classroom

Source: Creative Commons

"Part of grief is the loss of innocence. The loss of the certainty that
everything will always be as it has been."
-Tanya Lord

Professional Responsibility

Childcare centres and schools are a place where the majority of children spend a significant part of their lives and what children learn from educators may have long-term effects (Lowton & Higginson, 2003). Rowling and Holland (2000) state that society expects schools to support children in more than just their academic achievement; a universal goal for educators and schools is to care about the holistic development of each student, and sometimes that includes supporting children through the grieving process (Lawhon, 2004). Children spend a great deal of time in childcare or school and educators can be an important source of support for a grieving child (Fiorelli, 2002).

It is important for educators working with grieving children to understand the manifestation of grief at various developmental stages and to provide competent support to children of all ages who experience loss (McGuinness, 2011). Undoubtedly, many educators may be appropriately perceived as an important contact in a child's bereavement experience at a time when parents may be under substantial emotional pressure.

A concern educators often encounter is whether they have the skills necessary to work with children who are grieving (Doka, 2010). Cullinan (1990) who studied educator's death anxiety and perceived capability to support bereaved children, determined that the support children receive depends on the educator's perception of his or her role as an aid in the grieving process and his or her perceived comfort in dealing with death-related issues. Papadatou et al. (2002) also explored the perceptions of educators about children's adjustment to death, and the educator's personal experiences with a student who was grieving the death of a parent. Most participants perceived their role in supporting a bereaved student as significant, but a large majority felt unprepared to take on such a responsibility (Papadatou et al., 2002).

Although there are qualified specialists in the field of grief and bereavement counselling who are prepared to assume such a responsibility, what a grieving child needs more than anything else, is to be listened to and soothed by a caring and empathetic individual with whom the child interacts on a daily basis (Doka, 2010). Educators are uniquely positioned to guide grieving children because the classroom may be the primary setting in which children begin to cope with personal reactions to loss. The classroom can provide the continuity and security of a safe place that a grieving child may need to express his or her grief and talk about his or her loss (Naierman, 1997).

Death and Loss in the Curriculum

Loss, death, and dying should be addressed in school curriculum the same way we teach about character and moral education. Pinar (1992) suggests that the "concept and realities of death need to be integrated in everyday conversation and in everyday curriculum, and not treated as exotic topics of extreme anxiety" (p. 99). Similarly,

Crase and Crase (1977) suggest that if the goal of education is to contribute to a child's overall well-being, then death education should be a part of the process.

By nature, death and dying education can be taught using a multidisciplinary approach. It can be included in various subjects and experiences including Social Studies and Science. Educators can talk about the cycle of life and death with a classroom pet, when planting flowers, or event adopting caterpillars that turn into butterflies.

The curriculum can also be designed in a way that supports children who are grieving a loss. Willis (2002) states that children can learn to verbally and non-verbally express their feelings; therefore, young children can benefit from using art as a method to talk about loss, death, and dying. This book provides a variety of play-based activities that support death education in the curriculum, as well as activities that support children through the grieving process.

CULTURAL AND RELIGIOUS PRACTICES AND BELIEFS

Recognizing that there can be different patterns of mourning presents unique challenges to educators in understanding what normal and acceptable behaviour is for grieving children and families (Lopez, 2011). Cultural and religious variations in grief require educators to have the knowledge and skills to support children and families with different backgrounds than their own (Sheikh, 1998). Educators should feel compelled to learn about the bereaved family's religious traditions, but there are two challenges to this.

First, educators have a responsibility to listen to families and support their religious beliefs about grief and educators also have an obligation to support children. This can be challenging for educators because Christian, Buddhist, Hindu and Islamic families may expect children to refrain from grieving shortly after the child has lost a parent, but the educator may want to encourage parentally bereaved children to express their grief. Second, an educator's responsibility to learn about another religion and facilitate certain rituals in the classroom may be a difficult task if the religion is significantly different from the educator's personal religion. It is debatable whether or not educators should feel obligated to talk about death in light of another religion if they do not feel comfortable doing so; however, if educators do not collaborate with bereaved parents and provide support for parentally bereaved children in a way that is consistent with the child's religion, the educator may not be providing adequate support.

With the increasing diversity of society, educators may have children with a wide array of cultural and spiritual backgrounds in the classroom. Educators must recognize that many religions and cultures hold different end-of-life practices and beliefs about death, death rituals, and grieving. Sensitivity to different cultures' response patterns to death can help educators support children through the grieving process after the death of a parent. Educators cannot be expected to become an expert on every culture, but gaining a basic familiarity with the religions of the families within the community and knowing where to locate experts in these areas allows educators to provide optimal care to parentally bereaved children and their families.

The family is the best source of information for culturally sensitive assessment; therefore, educators should be comfortable asking families whether there are particular customs and rituals surrounding death and grief that they wish to share with the child care centre. By asking and listening to remaining family members, educators can obtain information and assess and integrate that information into the classroom's framework in a way that is culturally sensitive and family specific. By assessing and facilitating culturally appropriate grieving practices, educators can promote a healthy grieving process (Clements, Vigil, Manno & Henry, 2003; Ross, 2001).

INVOLVE PARENTS

Educators can better assist children through the grieving process when educators and parents interact together. This interaction aids in establishing a bond between the educator and parent and it provides educators with relevant facts that can be useful in supporting the grieving child (Lawhon, 2004). "They always talk to me about if they notice things, like if Laura has been quiet...They're very mindful on mother's day. They say, 'How do you want us to handle this? Should we make something for grandmas or for the girls?' And I always say, you know what, let's make it very organic. Let them choose. Let's not make such a big thing out of it." (Jones, 2012).
Educators can also connect with parents when they do not know how to respond to the children's questions or stories. "A couple of times Sophia has said, 'My mommy had a disease and she walked to the house and climbed on the tree and put a rope around her neck' which freaks the teachers out...it's freaky for [the teachers]. They are moms...It's a very heavy duty thing when that happens and I think they feel so much empathy for the kids and their hearts just really go out to them...They have been very kind and accommodating." (Jones, 2012).

OVERCOME TABOOS

Bowen (2002) asserted, "Chief among all taboo subjects is death" (p. 322). Educators' attitudes towards death are not different from the attitudes commonly held by adults in Western culture. Such attitudes typically include anxiety and are characterized by the automatic impulse to protect children from death-related events. Another barrier is the glorification of childhood, a period of life void of any pain or sorrow; therefore, shielding children from the morbid aspects of life is preferred more than helping children to develop coping abilities (Ayalon, 1979). However, as Kastenbaum (2000) states, "Nobody comes to an understanding of life without coming to some kind of understanding of death, and this process begins earlier than most of us imagined" (p. 6).

Mehraby (2003) advises that bereaved individuals should be allowed to express feelings of grief because suppressing them is damaging. The loss has to be acknowledged, the different emotions of grief have to be expressed, new skills may need to be developed, and a new approach to life must be focused on. Mehraby (2003) also states that bereavement is an upsetting and traumatic experience and it might comfort the mourner to know that such reactions and feelings are universal responses to loss. Shock, disbelief, denial, anger, guilt, bargaining, depression, and acceptance are common human reactions to the loss of a loved one. However, the duration, frequency, and intensity of the grief process may vary based on individual family and cultural beliefs (Walsh, King, Jones, Tookman & Blizard, 2002). As a result, culture is a complex but vital considerations in the process of helping people overcome death.

AVOID SILENCE: TALK TO CHILDREN ABOUT DEATH

"One universal goal for teachers and schools is to care about the overall development of each student" (Lawhon, 2004, p. 559). Educators are role models for students, but like many people in society, educators often feel uncomfortable discussing death and loss. This reluctance can affect children because they look to teachers for truth, knowledge, and support (Naierman, 1997).

Death is not necessarily depressing or frightening for children (Ayalon, 1979); however, children need accurate information about death in order for them to recognize, normalize, and discuss their grief concerns, providing children with a sense that death can be managed and it should not overwhelm them (Dowdney, 2008). Children have fears, fantasies, and questions; therefore, they need educators to listen to them, not minimize their concerns, and provide them with facts. Educators should also ensure they are acknowledging and respecting the children's feelings.

At any stage, it is important for educators to be open and honest with their child. It is common for educators to want to wait for the "right time", however, the longing for the "right time" comes from an internal desire to protect children from a scary reality.

Harpham (1997) wrote, "The greatest gift you can give your children is not protection from change, loss, pain or stress, but the condense and tools to cope and grow with all that life has to offer them" (p 223). Death is a taboo topic that most adults struggle to discuss, add children to the picture, and it makes a very uncomfortable conversation. When discussing the death or loss of a parent, responding to a child with "I don't know" and "That's a great question, I will try to find an answer" are acceptable and can in fact build strong rapports because of the level of honesty and trust (Seccareccia and Warnick, 2008).

Heath et al. (2008) add that half-truths or avoiding the topic are detrimental to healing and mourning in the long run. When sharing information with children, it is essential not to use euphemisms and terminology that can confuse children. When talking to children about death, it is important for educators to use the correct language such as *dead, killed, cancer*, and *suicide* (Fitzgerald, 2003). Using the correct language in such a way that children do not feel death is a taboo or unspeakable subject provides children an opportunity to begin accepting the finality of death (Willis, 2002). To illustrate, if Mom is dying/ has died because of Cancer, it is essential to use the "Cancer" word as opposed to saying, "Mom is sick/ill" (Seccareccia & Warnick, 2008). Using terminology such as ill/sick can lead children to associate having a cold with the possibility of dying (Seccareccia & Warnick, 2008).

Moreover, the response from the educator and/or caregiver should be one that encourages a supportive environment that allows the child to feel comfortable enough to talk about their feelings; statements such as "This must be really tough", "I am here for you" and "I need your help to understand what you are feeling and thinking" encourage children and allow them to be heard through emotional expression and body language (Heath et. al, 2008). Depending on the age group and personality of the child, it may be difficult to express their grief, worries, and fears. Allow children to know that you are available and would like to assist in a manner that is comfortable and acceptable to them (Heath et. al, 2008).

- When children ask: "What is death?"

- Educators can say: "When people die, their bodies stop working. They can't see, hear, feel eat, or breathe anymore. When a person's body stops working, it will never start working again. The person can never come back"

GIVE INVITING NONVERBAL CUES

For children, comfort comes from physical gestures; holding, hugging, snuggling. Therefore, it is important for educators to spend time simply sitting next to or hugging the child (Wolfelt, 2013).

When talking about death or the child's grief, it is important to be aware of your tone and make eye contact. With warmth and sincerity, you are sending the message to the child that he/she is okay and should freely express his/her feelings (Wolfelt, 2013).

It is also important to honour how children best express themselves. Sometimes children express themselves through drawing, writing in a journal, singing, dancing, crafts, or taking pictures. Create opportunities for children to express in a way that is comfortable for them (Wolfelt, 2013).

THERAPEUTIC ACTIVITIES

Circle of Control

AGES
4-12 years

DESCRIPTION
Any loss creates a sense of loss of control for children. Depending on the age, many children think they have caused the loss (death, divorce, etc). This activity provides an opportunity for children to visually see and understand the difference between what we can and cannot control.

MATERIALS
Chart paper
Markers

IMPLEMENTATION
On a poster or chart paper, have the children draw a large circle. Next, ask them to draw a smaller circle within the larger one. In the large circle, have the children list some things in life that are not within their control. For example, their parents, their hair colour, their health, etc. Within the smaller circle, have the children list some things that they can control. For example, their thoughts, their attitudes, being responsible, the words they use, etc.

ADAPTATIONS
For younger children, you may want to provide them with pictures or magazines, so that they can cut and paste pictures that represent what they can/cannot control rather than writing them out.

Adapted from: FranklinCovey Education. (n.d.). *The Leader in Me*. Retrieved from https://foxhollowsevenhabits.weebly.com/uploads/8/4/5/7/8457988/circle_of_control.pdf

Reflective Journal

AGES
10-12 years

DESCRIPTION
For many children, it is difficult to express emotions as a result of loss. A reflective journal allows children to translate their own thoughts and feelings into words, which helps them better understand themselves and how they feel, as well as their own thought processes. Children can also look back on how they were feeling on previous days, and look for signs of progress as time goes by. If children are comfortable with sharing their reflective journal with the adults in their lives, it provides an opportunity for discussion about thoughts, feelings, and fears.

MATERIALS
notebooks/journals
Pens/pencils

IMPLEMENTATION
On a daily or weekly basis, have the child(ren) find a spot within the environment where they can be alone and concentrate on writing in their journal.

ADAPTATIONS
This activity can be modified or simplified for younger ages, or for children who are having a difficult time thinking about what to write, by giving them a writing prompt each day/week, on areas to focus on.

Source: Merenda

Dreamcatchers

AGES
4-12 years

DESCRIPTION
Dreamcatchers are traditionally believed to protect children from bad dreams and nightmares. Disrupted sleep is common for children who have experienced a loss. This activity allows children to feel a sense of control over their sleep and emotions because they can create something believed to reduce negative emotions and thoughts at bedtime.

MATERIALS
metal ring
leather lace
beads
sinew/yarn

IMPLEMENTATION
First start off by explaining to the child what dreamcatchers are, and what they are used for. Brainstorm with the child the negative emotions, triggers, or experiences that may cause disruptions in their sleep.
Next, have them make their own dreamcatcher. 1.Fold a long piece of leather in half. Knot it to create a loop to hand the dreamcatcher. 2. Wrap each side of the leather tightly around the ring. The ends should meet at the bottom of the ring. Tie the ends in a knot. 3. Take the sinew or yarn and knot the end at the top of the ring near the loop. Move 1 inch along the loop and wrap the sinew/yarn loosely from the front to the back to create a loop. Continue until you get to the top of the ring again. 4. For each round, wrap the sinew/yarn around the middle of the stitch from the previous round. 5. Continue until you end of the bottom. 6. Have the children put beads on the loose ends of the leather lacing and knot the bottom.

Childhood Loss and Grief

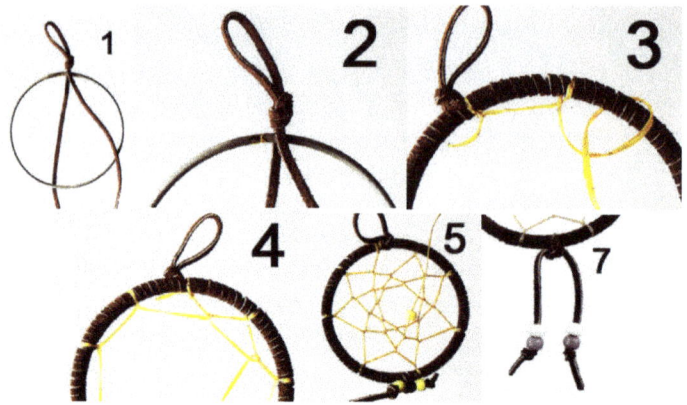

Adapted from: The Wandering Bull, LLC. (2019). *Dreamcatcher instructions*. Retrieved from https://wanderingbull.com/dreamcatcher-instructions/

My Family Portrait

AGES
4-12 years

DESCRIPTION
Divorce or the death of a parent affects every aspect of a child's life. One of the biggest and most obvious changes for children is the change in family dynamics. This activity encourages children to understand the new family structure, to be proud of their family, and to understand the various family dynamics.

MATERIALS
magazines
scissors
glue
construction paper
markers/crayons

IMPLEMENTATION
Begin by talking to the child(ren) about different family structures. As a group, you can brainstorm multiple kinds of families (you can give the child a visual representation with books, images etc.). Discuss the fact that family structures are unique to everyone, and family dynamics can always change but the love they have for their families and the love their families have for them does not change.
Provide children with various art materials including paint, crayons, magazines, and loose parts so that they can design a portrait of their new family dynamics.
This may lead into a discussion around how things have changed and how that makes the child feel.

Source: Merenda

Stress Balls

AGES
4-12 years

DESCRIPTION
Stress balls are a great home-made stress reliever for children. Stress balls are an easy craft to put together and can be created multiple different ways. Stress balls are meant to be small enough to fit in your hand, and can be used when someone is anxious, stressed, angry, etc. by squeezing it to relieve tension, and stress.

MATERIALS
beads/beans/sand/rice/rocks/flour etc.
balloon

IMPLEMENTATION
1. Stretch out your balloon
2. Choose your filling: rice, flour, sand, etc
3. Stick a funnel into the neck of the balloon
4. Slowly fill the balloon with the filling of choice
5. Remove the funnel from the balloon and let out as much air as you can
6. Tie the neck of the balloon tightly

Source: Merenda

Chapter Eight: Responding to Grieving Children in the Classroom

Balloon of Worries

AGES
4-12 years

DESCRIPTION
This activity allows children to identify and acknowledge their thoughts, feelings, and anything that is worrying or scaring them. They can literally and figuratively release those feeling to allow for healing and positive thought.

MATERIALS
balloons
pencils/crayons
small pieces of paper (small enough to slide into a balloon)
helium

IMPLEMENTATION
Before the activity begins, have the children discuss worry-what it is, what it can look like, and how it affects us. Then ask the children about certain things that make them upset/worried. Then have them write it down or draw it on a small piece of paper. Fill the balloon with the paper. Fill the balloon with helium. Then talk about the importance of recognizing and acknowledging scary or worrying feelings, but that it's also important to let them go so that we can fill ourselves with positive thoughts and healing. Release the balloon(s) for a visual demonstration.

Adapted from: *Art of Social Work*. (2019). *Worry balloons art*. Retrieved from https://kristinamarcelli.wordpress.com/2015/01/07/worry-balloons/

Storybooks

AGES
6-12 years

DESCRIPTION
It may be difficult to express and discuss the emotions that come with experiencing a loss. In most cases, it's difficult for children to express these emotions with others. This activity provides children an opportunity to come up with their own characters, settings, plot, problem, and most importantly, a solution. Writing a book gives the child a sense of control over what is happening in their story. It also allows them to fantasize and feel a sense of control- which is lost with any loss. Although children may not have any control over their real-life circumstance, they are given the opportunity of creating a story, coming up with characters, a problem, and then finding a solution to it. This activity gets children to think critically about problems, and how those problems can then be solved in the end.

MATERIALS
notebook
pencils/erasers
pencil crayons/crayons

IMPLEMENTATION
Without setting expectations around the time line for completion, have the children write a story. The children should be encouraged to come up with their own story line and plot. They can work together and ask questions about how to solve problems and conflicts that develop in their stories. Upon completion, allow them to share their book with others.

Source: Merenda

Chapter Eight: Responding to Grieving Children in the Classroom

Shield of Strength

AGES
6-12 years

DESCRIPTION
Children who are experiencing a loss often feel alone. They need to be reminded of the support systems that they have in their lives, even when it feels like they have no one to turn to. This activity allows children to identify the people who can support them. Creating a shield of strength encourages children to recognize the people in their lives who are there to help protect them and support them through the difficult events that happen in life.

MATERIALS
shield printout/ or cut out of a shield
scissors
pencil crayons/crayons

IMPLEMENTATION
Talk to the children about some of the difficult things that may happen to us or around us. Then talk about how important it is to ask for help when we need it and to rely on our support systems. Allow the children to decorate their shields with pictures and/or words that represent their own support systems and the people in their lives who are there to protect them and support them.

Adapted from: Hope 4 Hurt. (2018). *The Shield of Strength*. Retrieved from https://hope4hurtingkids.com/grief/shield-of-strength/

Worry Jar

AGES
4-12 years

DESCRIPTION
The worry jar is a great tool to have children recognize and acknowledge their worries. A worry jar is a helpful way to initiate a conversation with children, about their worries. Placing their thoughts in the jar will help them see their worries trapped away and also off their mind, at least for a little while.

MATERIALS
glass or plastic jar
different colour post-it notes

IMPLEMENTATION
Allow children some time to think about their own worries, identify them, and then write them or draw them on post-it notes to be put inside the worry jar. The children can either keep their worry jars if they'd like to revisit their worries, reflect on them, and talk about them. Or, they can give their worry jars away to symbolize releasing their worries.

Source: Merenda

Divorce Sentence Prompt

AGES
6-12 years

DESCRIPTION
Divorce is a hard topic for children to talk about. Children of divorced parents can have a hard time processing their feelings and thoughts about their parents' divorce. Sometimes these unexpressed emotions and thoughts have a negative impact on a child's academic performance and behaviour. This divorce sentence completion activity is designed to get kids talking in a non-threatening manner. When children do sentence completions, they often reveal more about what they are feeling, thinking, and/or experiencing as opposed to when they are asked direct questions.

MATERIALS
question cards ("The changes in my family makes me feel…", "Being in my family is like…", " I want my mom and dad to know…" etc.

IMPLEMENTATION
This activity can be done individually or in small groups. Have the children go through each question card and come up with an answer for it. They can use their answers to better understand how much they understand about divorce, and their own personal feelings and attitudes about it as well.

Adapted from: Teachers Pay Teachers. (n.d.). *Divorce Sentence Completion Activity.* Retrieved from https://www.teacherspayteachers.com/Product/Divorce-Sentence-Completion-Activity-2255573

Memory Box

AGES
4-12 years

DESCRIPTION
A memory box is a great way for children to special items that remind them of a loved one who has died. These items can relate directly to a loved one or can resemble the relationship the child shared with them.

MATERIALS
box (cardboard/wooden)
items (collected by child)
loose parts
paint
crayons/markers

IMPLEMENTATION
Begin by discussing the reasoning for the memory box and what kind of items they can include inside, to help them remember their loved one and remember the relationship they shared. The child can then decorate the box with paint, crayons, and/or loose parts and place the items they collected inside.

Remind the child that this box is there to help them remember their loved one. They can look inside the box when they are feeling sad or having a hard day, or, when they are just wanting to bring back memories they shared with that person.

Source: Merenda

Emotions Bingo

AGES
6-12 years

DESCRIPTION
This activity focuses on expressing and understanding feelings. Its aim is to increase a child's ability to verbally and non-verbally express and identify a variety of emotions.

MATERIALS
digital camera
printer
legal-size paper
glue
coloured photocopier
BINGO dabbers

IMPLEMENTATION
Begin by taking a picture of each child expressing a variety of emotions (angry, sad, happy, surprised, shy, sneaky, etc.). Using the pictures, create a class "Emotions BINGO" card. This will be done by printing out each picture and gluing them onto a piece of paper. Once the master copy is complete, photocopy enough cards for each child. The game is played like regular BINGO however, instead of calling out numbers the educator will call out emotions. To get a BINGO, a child must correctly identify the emotions being called and in doing so create a horizontal, diagonal, or vertical line on their BINGO sheet. The game can be followed by a discussion about times when children felt those emotions.

Source: Merenda

Colour My Feelings

AGES
4-9 years

DESCRIPTION
This activity focuses on expressing and identifying feelings. During this activity, children are able to depict feelings in an artistic way using colours.

MATERIALS
large paper
marker
crayons

IMPLEMENTATION
Begin by tracing the child's body onto a large sheet of paper. Ask the child to colour their body with a colour that represents a specific feeling. For example, they might colour their body to represent how you feel when you are sad.

This can be done multiple times with the same child using a variety of emotions. Once the children are done colouring, the outlines can be labelled with the emotion they represent and displayed around the classroom.

Source: Merenda

Problem Solver

AGES
6-12 years

DESCRIPTION
This activity provides children with an opportunity to develop solutions to problems their peers are currently facing.

MATERIALS
box
writing utensils
paper

IMPLEMENTATION
Each week, one child will be given the title of "Problem Solver". Throughout the week, children will have an opportunity to anonymously write down any problems they are facing on a piece of paper and place it inside the box. At the end of the week, the Problem Solver will read each problem aloud to their peers. After, they will give their advice on how they would solve the problem. Additionally, the problem Solver will call on his/her their peers to offer additional solutions to the problem. You should only direct the conversation if the children begin to give advice which may not be of any benefit or is counterproductive to the problem.

Source: Merenda

What I Like About You

AGES
6-12 years

DESCRIPTION
Childhood loss, including childhood illness, can be alienating. Children may feel different from their peers. Long-term hospital stays or taking time off from school after a loved one's death can effect children's relationships in the classroom. This activity encourages connection and friendship amongst peers.

IMPLEMENTATION
Ask the children to sit in a circle. Begin by reading a book about friendship to set the tone for the discussion. You can then discuss the challenges that occur within friendships when a child is away from school for long periods of time for any given reason. The story and discussion is then followed by an activity where each child says something that they like about the friend siting on their right/left, and why.

Source: Merenda

A Letter to My Future Self

AGES
6-12 years

DESCRIPTION
Grief is difficult for anyone, but especially for children. Loss leaves us with so much uncertainty about the present and future. This activity provides children an opportunity to express their worries about the future by writing down their thoughts and emotions in a positive and private way. When children can translate their own thoughts and feelings into words, it helps them better understand themselves and how they feel, as well as their own thought processes.

MATERIALS
sheet of paper
pens/pencils
envelopes

IMPLEMENTATION
Ask the children to write a letter to their future self. Have them write down what they hope their future self will be doing and achieving in a years-time. Tell the children to write about how they are currently feeling, what life is like for them at the moment, and what they are experiencing. They should also reflect on what they would like to happen for things to be better in their lives. Then, have the child seal the letter in an envelope. Depending on their age, ask the children or their parents to keep the letter sealed for a year. Through this activity children will be focused on thinking about the future and the kinds of goals they want to work towards instead of their present worries

Source: Merenda

Sensory Bottle

AGES
3-12 years

DESCRIPTION
This activity allows children to create a self-regulating tool that they can use when they are feeling overwhelmed. Sensory bottles can be used when a child is experiencing an overwhelming feeling, and they need time to calm down.

MATERIALS
clear hair gel
warm water
a tall bottle
loose parts
glitter
super glue or tape to secure lid (optional)

IMPLEMENTATION
To make:
1. Combine 1 part hair gel to 6 parts **warm water.** Let cool completely and settle.
2. Pour gel/water mix into the bottle.
3. Add glitter and the child's choice of loose parts.
4. Fill the bottle **right to the very top** with the remaining mixture.
5. Put on lid, shake **vigorously** and test your bottle.
6. Secure the lid with a waterproof glue or wide, clear packaging tape

Source: Merenda

Chapter Eight: Responding to Grieving Children in the Classroom

Worry Kit

AGES
6-12 years

DESCRIPTION
This activity is based on the book called *What to Do When You Worry Too Much* by Dawn Huebner. This book goes through several ways that can help kids manage anxiety, including setting a time for worries, thinking about things that make you happy and resetting your body with activity or relaxation. There are some interactive places in this book, where a child can write down their worries, draw some images of things that might help, etc. The worry kit is a great follow up activity that allows children to use some of the coping strategies presented in this book and create their own worry kit, equipped with all the things they might need when their worries get too big.

MATERIALS
box
objects of the child's choice

IMPLEMENTATION
Begin by reading *What to Do When You Worry Too Much*. When you have finished reading the book, ask the children about their own worries. Ask them as well about some of the things they do when they start to feel worried or overwhelmed. Each child can then create a worry kit including some things that help the child handle their worries in a positive way. For example, if "talk to grandma" is one strategy, the child can add the grandmother's number in the kit with a note about why or how the grandma helps the child when they are worried.

Source: Merenda

Pet Keepsakes

AGES
3-9 years

DESCRIPTION
Many children experience grief for the first time when their pet dies. Regardless if the pet was a family dog or a goldfish, children dealing with grief experience grief just as intensely as they would if it was a human family member. This activity allows children to make a keepsake to remember their pet.

MATERIALS
clay

IMPLEMENTATION
Children can use the clay to make a keepsake that reminds them of their pet. Some examples include a paw print or a name tag.

Source: Merenda

Chapter Eight: Responding to Grieving Children in the Classroom

Exploding Hearts

AGES
4-12 years

DESCRIPTION
Many children who have experienced a loss do not know how to communicate or express the feelings that they are experiencing inside. This activity allows the child to develop some self-awareness and help them deal with emotions that can be overwhelming.

MATERIALS
paper bags
crayons
stones/rocks

IMPLEMENTATION
Begin by having the children decorate a paper bag to represent their heart. Then ask them to think about a time when they were angry, scared or worried. Ask them to add a hand full of stones/rocks into the bag, representing the angry, scared or worried feeling in their body. Have them think about another time when they were angry, scared or worried and ask them to add a hand full of stones/rocks into the bag representing *that* feeling in their body. This is repeated using a variety of situations that they can think of as they continue filling their bag/heart.
Eventually the bag will overfill. Then ask the child to explain why they think the bag is overfilled.

Ask the child:
What happens when we hold onto angry, scary and worried feelings for too long? How does it make you act? Empty the bag and complete the activity again, except this time, have them talk about the feelings each time they fill their bag. Once they have spoked about it, ask them to remove half a hand full of rocks/stones. Ask them what is different about this activity. Continue the conversation until the child to acknowledges that talking to someone and about their feelings is an important coping strategy.

Source: Merenda

Memory Bracelets

AGES
4-12 years

DESCRIPTION
This activity is appropriate for children of many ages, as it encourages positive memories and coping.

MATERIALS
string
different kinds of beads

IMPLEMENTATION
Provide the child with different colour/size/ and kind of beads. Then ask them to add a specific bead that answers the following questions:
Add a bead to represent the loved ones favourite colour
Add a bead to represent the loves ones favourite holiday
Add a bead to represent the loved ones birth month
Add a bead to represent the loves ones favourite season
Add a bead to represent the happiest memory with your loved one
Add a bead to represent the love you have for your loved one

Source: Merenda

Chapter Eight: Responding to Grieving Children in the Classroom

Blow Bubbles

AGES
3-9 years

DESCRIPTION
Blowing bubbles is a great to teach children to breathe deeply, which is an easy coping and calming strategy for children.

MATERIALS
bubble blowing kit

IMPLEMENTATION
Begin by demonstrating how to breathe deeply and blow to create bubbles. It is important to highlight how deep breathing impacts their body, and how it can train the body to relax. Encourage children to practice their deep breathing skills by blowing their own bubbles.

Adapted from: Therapy Source. (2017). *Activities for Treating Anxiety in Children*. Retrieved from:
https://txsource.com/2017/06/30/8-activities-treating-anxiety-children/

REFERENCES

Abrams, R. (1999). *When parents die* (2nd ed.). London: Routledge.
Ahmad, W. D. (1996). An Islamic view of death and dying. *Journal of the Islamic Medical Association of North America, 28*, 175-177. Retrieved from http://scholarlyexchange.org/ojs/index.php/JIMA/article/viewFile/8091/28_4-7
Aiken, L. (2001). *Dying, death, and bereavement.* New Jersey: Lawrence Erlbaum Associates, Inc.
Alisic, E., Groot, A., Snetselaar, H., Stroeken, T., & Van De Putte, E. (2015). Parental intimate partner homicide and its consequences for children: Protocol for a population-based study. *BMC Psychiatry, 15*(1), 177. doi: 10.1186/s12888-015-0565-z
Alisic, E., Krishna, R., Groot, A., & Frederick, J. (2015). Children's mental health and well-being after parental intimate partner homicide: A systematic review. *Clinical Child and Family Psychology Review, 18*(4), 328-345. doi: 10.1007/s10567-015-0193-7
Armstrong-Dailey, A. (1991). *Hospice care for children: Their families and health care providers.* New York, NY: Hemisphere Publishing Co.
Auman, M. (2007). Bereavement support for children. *The Journal of School Nursing, 23*(1), 34-39.
Ayalon, O. (1979). Is death a proper subject for the classroom? Comments on death education. *International Journal of Social Psychiatry, 25*(4), 252-257.
Bank, R., & Wiggins, J. (2005). *101 things everyone should know about Judaism: Beliefs, practices, customs.* Massachusetts: Media, Inc.
Bluebond-Langner, M. (1978). *The private worlds of dying children.* Princeton, NJ: Princeton University Press.
Bowen, M. (1978). *Family therapy in clinical practice.* London: Aronson.
Bowlby, J. (1960). Grief and mourning in infancy and early childhood. *Psychoanalytic Study of the Child, 15*, 9-52.
Bowlby, J. (1980). *Loss: Sadness and depression.* New York: Basic Books.
Boyd, D., Johnson, P., & Bee, H. (2012). *Lifespan development.* Toronto: Pearson Canada Inc.
Breidenstein, A. (2002). Researching teaching, researching self: Qualitative research and beginning teacher development. *The Clearing House, 75*(6), 314-318.
Bricher, G. (2000). Children in the hospital: Issues of power and vulnerability. *Pediatric Nursing, 26*(3), 277.
Buckle, J., Dwyer, S., & Jackson, M. (2009). Qualitative bereavement research: Incongruity between the perspectives of participants and research ethics boards. *International Journal of Social Research Methodology, 13*(2), 111-125.
Burrell, L. V., Mehlum, L., & Qin, P. (2018). Sudden parental death from external causes and risk of suicide in the bereaved offspring: A national study. *Journal of Psychiatric Research, 96*, 49-56. doi: 10.1016/j.jpsychires.2017.09.023
Bylund-Grenklo, T., Fürst, C., Nyberg, T., Steineck, G., & Kreicbergs, U. (2016). Unresolved grief and its consequences. A nationwide follow-up of teenage loss of a parent to cancer 6–9 years earlier. *Supportive Care in Cancer, 24*(7), 3095-3103. doi: 10.1007/s00520- 016-3118-1
Cain, A., & Fast, I. (1966). Children's disturbed reactions to parent suicide. *American Journal of Orthopsychiatry, 36*(5), 873-880.
Canadian Cancer Society. (2012). *What is non-Hodgkin lymphoma?* Retrieved from http://www.cancer.ca/canada-wide/about%20cancer/types%20of%20cancer/what%20is%20non-hodgkin%20lymphoma.aspx
Charles, D. R., & Charles, M. (2006). Sibling loss and attachment style: An exploratory study. *Psychoanalytic Psychology, 23*(1), 72-90. doi: 10.1037/0736-9735.23.1.72

Chase, N. D. (1999). *Burdened children: Theory, research and treatment of parentification.* Thousand Oaks, CA: Sage Publications Inc.
Chittick, W. (1992). *Faith and practice of Islam: Three thirteenth century sufi text.* New York, NY: State University of New York Press.
Christ, G. H. (2000). *Healing children's grief: Surviving a parent's death from cancer.* New York, NY: Oxford University Press.
Clark, C. (2011). *In a younger voice: Doing child-centred qualitative research: Doing child-centred qualitative research. In a younger voice.* New York, NY: Oxford University Press.
Clarke-Stewart, A. & Brentano, C. (2006). *Divorce: Causes and consequences.* USA: Library of Congress Cataloging-in-Publication Data.
Clements, P., Vigil, G., Manno, M., & Henry, G. (2003). Cultural perspectives of death, grief, and bereavement. *Journal of Psychosocial Nursing and Mental Health Services, 41(7),* 18-26.
Coad, J., & Shaw, K. (2008). Is children's choice in health care rhetoric or reality? A scoping Review. *Journal of Advanced Nursing, 64*(4), 318-327.
Cobley, P. (2001). *Narrative.* London: Routledge.
Cohen, J., & Mannarino, A. (2011). Supporting children with traumatic grief: What educators need to know. *School Psychology International, 32(2),* 117-131.
Cohen, J., Mannarino, A., Greenberg, T., Padlo, S., & Shipley, C. (2002). Childhood traumatic grief: Concepts and controversies. *Trauma, Violence, & Abuse, 3*(4), 307-327.
Corr, C. A., & Balk, D. (2010). *Children's encounters with death, bereavement, and coping.* New York, NY: Springer Publishing Company.
Corr, C. A., & Corr, D. M. (1996). *Handbook of childhood death and bereavement.* New York, NY: Springer Publishing Company.
Costa, L., & Holliday, D. (1994). Helping children cope with the death of a parent. *Elementary School Guidance & Counseling 48*(3), 206-213.
Coyne, I. (2008). Children's participation in consultations and decision-making at health service level: A review of the literature. *International Journal of Nursing Studies, 45*(11), 1682-1689.
Crane, R., & Marshall, E. (2006). *Handbook of families and health.* California: Sage Publications Inc.
Crase, D. R., & Crase, D. (1985). Death education in the schools for older children. In H. Wass & C. A. Corr (Ed.), *Childhood and death* (pp. 345-361). New York: Hemisphere.
Cullinan, A. (1990). Teacher's death anxiety, ability to cope with death and perceived ability to aid bereaved students. *Death Studies, 14,* 147-160.
Curie, M. (2008). *Questions children may want to ask when someone close to them has died.* Retrieved from http://www.mariecurie.org.uk/Documents/PATIENTS-CAREERS-FAMILIES/Updated-pdf/question-children-ask-about-death.pdf
Cutcliffe, J. R. (1998). Hope, counselling and complicated bereavement reactions. *Journal of Advanced Nursing, 28*(4), 754-761. doi: 10.1046/j.1365-2648.1998.00724.x
Del Balso, M., & Lewis, A. D. (2001). Social survey. In (6th ed.), *First steps: A guide to social research* (pp. 97-127). Scarborough, ON: Nelson Thomson Learning.
Dennis, D. (2009). *Living, dying, grieving.* USA: Jones and Bartlett Publishers, LLC.
Deshpande, O., Reid, C., & Rao, A. (2005). Attitudes of Asian-Indian Hindus towards end-of-life care. *Journal of the American Geriatrics Society, 53*(1), 131-135.
Dodd, P., Guerin, S., McEvoy, J., Buckley, S., Tyrrell, J., & Hillery, J. (2008). A study of complicated grief symptoms in people with intellectual disabilities. *Journal of Intellectual Disability Research, 52*(5), 415-425. doi: 10.1111/j.1365-2788.2008.01043.x
Dodge, C. (2009). *The everything understanding Islam book.* MA: Adams Media.
Doka, K. (2000). *Living with grief: Children, adolescents, and loss.* United States of America: Hospice Foundation of America.
Doka, K. J. (1995). *Children mourning, mourning children.* New York, NY: Routledge.
Dowdney, L. (2008). Children bereaved by parent or sibling death. *Psychiatry, 7*(6), 270-275.

Duggan, D. D., Medway, F. J., & Bunke, V. L. (2004). Training educators to address the needs and issues of students with chronic illnesses: Examining their knowledge, confidence levels, and perceptions. *Canadian Journal of School Psychology, 19*(1-2), 149-165.

Dunning, S. (2006). As a young child's parent dies: Conceptualizing and constructing preventive interventions. *Clinical Social Work Journal, 34*(4), 499-514.

Dyregrov, A. (2008). *Grief in young children: A handbook for adults*. London: Jessica Kingsley Publishers.

Earley, L., & Cushway, D. (2002). The parentified child. *Clinical Child Psychology and Psychiatry, 7*(2), 163-178.

Edwards, C. (2000). *Handling death and bereavement at work*. Oxon: Gerald Duckworth & Co. Ltd.

Emery, R. E. (2004). *The truth about children and divorce*. New York, NY: Penguin Group.

Engelhardt, J. A. (2012). The developmental implications of parentification: Effects on childhood attachment. *Journal of Psychology, 14*, 45-52.

Eppler, C. (2008). Exploring themes of resiliency in children after the death of a parent. *Professional School Counseling, 11*(3), 189-196.

Fiorelli, R. (2002). Grief and bereavement in children. In Kinzbrunner, B., Weinreb, N., & Policzer, J. (2nd Ed.), *End-of-life-care: A practical guide* (pp. 635-665). United States: McGraw-Hill Companies.

Firth, S. (2005). End-of-life: a Hindu view. *The Lancet, 366*(9486), 682-686.

Fitzgerald, H. (2003). *The grieving children*. New York, NY: Fireside.

Fossey, E., Harvey, C., McDermott, F., & Davidson, L. (2002). Understanding and evaluating qualitative research. *Australian and New Zealand Journal of Psychiatry, 36*(6), 717-732.

Franklin, C., Harris, M., & Allen-Meares, P. (2006). *The school services sourcebook: A guide for school-based professionals*. New York, NY: Oxford University Press.

Fujisawa, D., Miyashita, M., Nakajima, S., Ito, M., Kato, M., & Kim, Y. (2010). Prevalence and determinants of complicated grief in general population. *Journal of Affective Disorders, 127*(1-3), 352-358. doi: 10.1016/j.jad.2010.06.008

Fulton, R. & Fulton, J. (1971). A psychosocial aspect of terminal care: Anticipatory grief. *OMEGA: The Journal of Death and Dying, 2*, 91-100.

Furman, E. (1974). *A child's parent dies*. New Haven, CT: Yale University Press.

Furst, B. (2007). Bowlby goes to the movies: Film as a teaching tool for issues of bereavement, mourning, and grief in medical education. *Academic Psychiatry, 31*(5), 407-410. doi: 10.1176/appi.ap.31.5.407

Furstenberg, F. F., & Cherlin, A. J. (1991). *Divided families: What happens to children when parents part*. USA: Library of Congress Cataloging in Publication Data.

Gale, D., Mitchel, A., Garand, L., & Wesner, S. (2003). Client narratives: A theoretical perspective. *Issues in Mental Health Nursing, 24*(1), 81-89.

Geis, H., Whittlesey, S., McDonald, N., Smith, K., & Pfefferbaum, B. (1998). Bereavement and loss in childhood. *Child and Adolescent Psychiatric Clinics of North America, 7*(1), 73-85.

Geller, J. (1985). The long-term outcome of unresolved grief: An example. *Psychiatric Quarterly, 57*(2), 142-146. doi: 10.1007/BF01064333

Gerring, J. (2007). *Case study research: Principles and practices*. New York: Cambridge University Press.

Given, L. (2008). *The sage encyclopedia of qualitative research methods* (2nd ed.). Thousand Oaks, CA: Sage.

Glazer, H., Clark, M., Thomas, R., & Haxton, H. (2010). Parenting after the death of a spouse. *American Journal of Hospice and Palliative Medicine, 27*(8), 532-536. doi: 10.1177/1049909110366851

Goldman, L. (2001). *Breaking the silence: A guide to help children with complicated grief-suicide, homicide, AIDS, violence, and abuse* (2nd ed.). New York: Guilford Press.

Grollman, E. (1995). *Bereaved children and teens: A support guide for parents and professionals*. Boston, MA: Beacon Press Books.

Guzzetta, C. (1998). *Essential readings in holistic nursing*. USA: Aspen Publishers, Inc.

Haine, R. A., Ayers, T. S., Sandler, I. N., & Wolchik, S. A. (2008). Evidence-based practices for parentally bereaved children and their families. *Professional Psychology, Research and Practice, 39*(2), 113–121. doi: 10.1037/0735-7028.39.2.113

Heath M. A., Leavy D., Hansen K., Ryan K., Lawrence L., & Sonntag A. G. (2008). Coping with grief: Guidelines and resources for assisting children. *Intervention in School and Clinic, 43*(5), 259-269.

Høeg, B. L., Johansen, C., Christensen, J., Frederiksen, K., Dalton, S. O., Dyregrov, A., Bidstrup, P. E. (2018). Early parental loss and intimate relationships in adulthood: A nationwide study. *Developmental Psychology, 15*(5), 963-974. doi: 10.1037/dev0000483

Holmes, J. (2014). *John Bowlby and attachment theory* (2nd ed.). New York, NY: Routledge

Hooyman, N., & Kramer, B. (2006). *Living through loss: Interventions across the lifespan*. New York, NY: Columbia University Press.

Hope, R., & Hodge, D. (2006). Factors affecting children's adjustment to the death of a parent: The social work professional's viewpoint. *Child and Adolescent Social work Journal, 23*(1), 107-126.

Howarth, R. (2011). Promoting the adjustment of parentally bereaved children. *Journal of Mental Health Counseling, 33*(1), 21-32.

Howell, K., Barrett-Becker, E., Burnside, A., Wamser-Nanney, R., Layne, C., & Kaplow, J. (2016). Children facing parental cancer versus parental death: The buffering effects of positive parenting and emotional expression. *Journal of Child and Family Studies, 25*(1), 152-164. doi: 10.1007/s10826-015-0198-3

Hung, N., & Rabin, L. (2009). Comprehending childhood bereavement by parental suicide: A critical review of research on outcomes, grief processes, and interventions. *Death Studies, 33*, 781-814.

Hunter, S., & Smith, D. (2008). Predictors of children's understandings of death: Age, cognitive ability, death experience and maternal communicative competence. *OMEGA, 57*(2), 143-162.

Huntley, T. (2002). *Helping children grieve: When someone they love dies*. Minneapolis, MN: Library of Congress Cataloging-in-Publication Data.

James, B. (1989). *Treating traumatized children: New insights and creative interventions*. New York, NY: The Free Press.

Johnson, H. (1993). Stressful family experiences and young children: How the classroom teacher can help. *Intervention in School and Clinic, 28*(3), 165-171.

Johnson, J. (1999). *Keys to helping children deal with death and grief*. New York: Barron's Educational Series, Inc.

Jordan, J. R. (2001). Is suicide bereavement different?: A reassessment of the literature. *Suicide and Life-Threatening Behaviour, 31*(1), 91-103.

Kalantari, M., & Vostanis, P. (2010). Behavioural and emotional problems in Iranian children four years after parental death in an earthquake. *International Journal of Social Psychiatry, 56*(2), 158-167. doi: 10.1177/0020764008101854

Kalter, N., Lohnes, K., Chasin, J., Cain, A., Dunning, S., & Rowan, J. (2002). The adjustment of parentally bereaved children: Factors associated with short-term adjustment. *OMEGA, 46*(1), 15-34.

Kaplan, S., & Shoenberg, L. (1988). Defining suicide: Importance and implications for Judaism. *Journal of Religion & Health, 27*(2), 154-156.

Kastenbaum, R. (2000). The kingdom where nobody dies. In K. J. Doka (Ed.), *Living with grief: Children, adolescents, and loss* (pp. 5-20). Washington, DC: Hospice Foundation of America.

Kenneth, D. (2010). *When kids are grieving: Addressing grief and loss in school*. California: Corwin.

Keown, D. (2005). End of life: The Buddhist view. *The Lancet, 366*(9489), 952-955.

Kubler-Ross, E. (1969). *On death and dying*. New York: Macmillan.

Kirwin, K. & Hamrin, V. (2005). Decreasing the risk of complicated bereavement and future psychiatric disorders in children. *Journal of Child and Adolescent Psychiatric Nursing, 18*(2), 62-78.

Koenig, H. G., & Shohaib, S. A. (2014). *Health and well-being in Islamic societies: Background, research, and applications*. Switzerland: Springer International Publishing.

Koller, D., Nicholas, D., Gearing, R., & Kalfa, O. (2010). Peadiatric pandemic planning: Children's perspectives and recommendations. *Health and Social Care in the Community, 18*(4), 369-377.

Komaromy, C. (2004). Cultural diversity in death and dying. *Nursing Management, 11*(8), 32-36.

Kroen, W. (1996). *Helping children cope with the loss of a loved one: A guide for grownups.* Minneapolis: Free Spirit Publishing Inc.

Krueger, D. W. (1983). Childhood parent loss: Developmental impact and adult psychopathology. *American Journal of Psychotherapy, 37*(4), 582-592.

Kuramoto, J., Brent, D., & Wilcox, H. (2009). The impact of parental suicide on child and adolescent offspring. *Suicide and Life-Threatening Behaviour, 39*(2), 137-151.

Kyle, T. (2008). *Essentials of pediatric nursing.* China: Lippincott Williams & Wilkins.

Lansdown, G. (2001). *Promoting children's participation in democratic decision-making.* Italy: Arti Grafiche.

Lasher, C. (2008). *Death is no stranger: Helping children grieve.* Lima, OH: CSS Publishing Company Inc.

Lawhon, T. (2004). Teachers and schools can aid grieving students. *Education, 124*(3), 559-566.

Lawrence, E., Jeglic, E. L., Matthews, L. T., & Pepper, C. M. (2006). Gender differences in grief reactions following the death of a parent. *Journal of Death & Dying, 52*(4), 323-337.

Lehman, D., Lang, E., Wortman, C., & Sorenson, S. (1989). Long-term effects of sudden bereavement: Marital and parent-child relationships and children's reactions. *Journal of Family Psychology, 2*(3), 344-367.

Lewis, P., & Lippman, J. (2004). *Helping children cope with the death of a parent.* USA: Greenwood Publishing Group, Inc.

Li, J., Vestergaard, M., Cnattingius, S., Gissler, M., Bech, B. H., Obel, C., . . . Olsen, J. (2014). Mortality after parental death in childhood: A nationwide cohort study from three Nordic countries. *PLOS Medicine, 11*(7), 17. doi: 10.1371/journal.pmed.1001679

Lindemann, E. (1944). The symptomology and management of acute grief. *American Journal of Psychiatry, 101,* 141-148.

Lobar, S., Youngblut, J., & Brooten, D. (2006). Cross-cultural beliefs, ceremonies, and rituals surrounding death of a loved one. *Pediatric Nursing, 32*(1), 44-50.

Lopez, S. (2011). Culture as an influencing factor in adolescent grief and bereavement. *The Prevention Researcher, 18*(3), 10-13.

Lowton, K., & Higginson, I. (2003). Managing bereavement in the classroom: A conspiracy of silence? *Death Studies, 27*(8), 717-741.

Maccallum, F., & Bryant, R. A. (2013). A cognitive attachment model of prolonged grief: Integrating attachments, memory, and identity. *Clinical Psychology Review, 33*(6), 713- 727. doi: 10.1016/j.cpr.2013.05.001

Mahathera, V. (2001). *The thirty-one planes of existence.* Malaysia: Inward Path.

Martenson, E. & Fagerskiold, A. (2007). A review of children's decision-making competence in health care. *Journal of Clinical Nursing, 17*(23), 3131-3141.

Martin, A., Volkmar, F. R., & Lewis, M. (2007). *Child and adolescent psychiatry: A comprehensive textbook.* Philadelphia, PA: Congress Cataloging-in-Publication Data.

Masao, F. (1983). Maintenance and change in Japanese traditional funerals and death-related behaviour. *Japanese Journal of Religious Studies, 10*(1), 39-64.

Matzo, M., & Sherman, D. (2010). *Palliative care nursing: Quality care to the end of life.* (3rd ed.). New York, NY: Springer Publishing Company.

McCabe, M. (1996). Involving children and adolescents in medical decision making: developmental and clinical considerations. *Journal of Pediatric Psychology, 21(4),* 505-516.

Mccall, J., & Koenig, H. (1999). *Grief education for caregivers of the elderly.* New York, NY: The Haworth Pastoral Press.

McClatchy, I., & Vonk, M. (2009). The prevalence of childhood traumatic grief - A comparison of violent/sudden and expected loss. *OMEGA, 59*(4), 305-323.

McGoldrick, M. (2004). Legacies of loss: Multigenerational ripple effects. In F. Walsh & M. McGoldrick (3rd Ed.), *Living beyond loss: Death in the family* (pp. 61-84). New York: W. W. Norton.

McGoldrick, M., Almeida, R., Hines, P. M., Gracia-Preto, N., Rosen, E., & Lee, E. (1991). Mourning in different cultures. In F. Walsh & M. McGoldrick (Ed.), *Living beyond loss: Death in the family* (pp. 176-206). New York: Norton.

McGuinness, T. (2011). Grief and loss of a caregiver in children. *Journal of Psychosocial Nursing, 49*(10), 17-20.

McNamara, C. (2009). *General guidelines for conducting interviews.* Retrieved from http://managementhelp.org/evaluatn/intrview.htm

Mehraby, N. (2003). Psychotherapy with Islamic clients facing loss and grief. *Psychotherapy in Australia, 9*(2), 1-8.

Melhem, N. M., Moritz, G., Walker, M., Shear, M., & Breant, D. (2007). Phenomenology and correlates of complicated grief in children and adolescents. *Journal of the American Academy of Child and Adolescent Psychiatry, 46*(4), 493-499.

Miller, A. C., Ziad-Miller, A., & Elamin, E. M. (2014, November 24). Brain death and Islam: The interface of religion, culture, history, law, and modern medicine. *Respiratory Therapeutics Week.* Retrieved from http://link.galegroup.com.subzero.lib.uoguelph.ca/apps/doc/A395049482/AONE?u=guel77241&sid=AONE&xid=658039fc

Mitchell, A. M., Kim, Y., Prigerson, H. G, & Martimer-Stephens, M. (2004). Complicated grief in survivors of suicide. *Crisis, 25*(1), 12-18.

Mongelluzzo, N. B. (2013). *Understanding loss and grief: A guide through life changing events.* Plymouth, UK: Rowman & Littlefield.

Monroe, B., & Kraus, F. (2010). *Brief interventions with bereaved children.* New York, NY: Oxford University Press.

Morgan, G. & Smircich, L. (1980). The Case for qualitative research. *The Academy of Management Review, 5*(4), 491-500.

Mount Sinai Hospital. (n.d.). *Special bereavement camp will welcome children this September.* Retrieved from http://www.mountsinai.on.ca/patients/our-stories/special- bereavement-camp-will-welcome-children-this-september

Murray, J. (2005). *Loss and grief for children in care.* St Lucia, AU: The University of Queensland.

Nagera, H. (1978). Children's reactions to hospitalization and illness. *Child Psychiatry and Human Development, 9*(1), 3-19.

Naierman, N. (1997). Reaching out to grieving students. *Educational Leadership, 55*(2), 62-65.

Neuman, W. L. (2006). *Social research methods: Qualitative and quantitative approaches.* Toronto, ON: Pearson Education Inc.

Nickman, S., Silverman, P., & Normand, C. (1998). Children's construction of a deceased parent: The surviving parent's contribution. *American Journal of Orthopsychiatry, 68*(1), 126-134.

Noppe, I. C. (2000). Beyond broken bonds and broken hearts: The bonding of theories of attachment and grief. *Developmental Review, 20*(4), 514- 538. doi: 10.1006/drev.2000.0510

Noyes, J. (2000). Enabling young 'ventilator-dependent' people to express their views and experiences of their care in hospital. *Journal of Advanced Nursing, 31*(5), 1206-1215.

Ostrowki, T. M., Sikorska, I., & Gerc, K. (2015). *Resilience and health: In a fast- changing world.* Krakow, PL: Jagiellonian University Press.

Papadatou, D., Metallinou, O., Hatzichristou, C., & Pavlidi, L. (2002). Supporting the bereaved child: Teacher's perceptions and experiences in Greece. *Mortality, 7*(3), 324-339.

Perkins, H., Cortez, J., & Hazuda, H. (2009). Cultural beliefs about a patient's right time to die: An exploratory study. *Society of General Internal Medicine, 24*(11), 1240-1247.

Pfeffer, C. (1981). Parental suicide: An organizing event in the development of latency age children. *Suicide and Life-Threatening Behaviour, 11,* 43-50.

References

Pfeffer, C. R., Karus, D., Siegel, K., & Jiang, H. (2000). Child survivors of parental death from cancer or suicide: Depressive and behavioral outcomes. *Psycho-Oncology, 9*(1), 1-10. doi: 10.1002/(SICI)1099-1611(200001/02)9:1<1:AID-PON430>3.0.CO;2-5

Pidcock, B., Ashpole, B., & Warnick, A. (2015). *Report to the children and youth grief collaborative services for children and youth, grief and bereavement Region of Peel.* Retrieved from http://hearthousehospice.com/wp-content/uploads/2014/08/ChildrenYouthGriefFINALNeeds Assessment.pdf

Pinar, W. F., & Reynolds, W. M. (1992). *Understanding curriculum as a phenomenological and deconstructed text.* New York, NY: Teachers College Press.

Pomeroy, E., & Garcia, R. B. (2009). *The grief assessment and intervention workbook: A strengths perspective.* Belmont, CA: Brooks/Cole.

Porterfield, K., Cain, A., & Saldinger, A. (2003). The impact of early loss history on parenting of bereaved children: A qualitative study. *Omega: Journal or Death and Dying, 47*(3), 203-220. doi: 10.2190/FL59-Q4E3-3NBE-2XGJ

Price, D. L., & Gwin, J. F. (2008). *Pediatric Nursing: An Introductory Text.* St. Louise, MS: Saunders Elsevier.

Puchalski, C., & O'Donnell, E. (2005). Religious and spiritual beliefs in end of life care: How major religions view death and dying. *Techniques in Regional Anesthesia and Pain Management, 9*(3), 114-121.

Rando, T. (1984). *Grief, dying, and death: Clinical interventions for caregivers.* Illinois: Research Press.

Raveis, V. H., Siegel, K., & Karus, D. (1999). Children's psychological distress following the death of a parent. *Journal of Youth and Adolescence, 28*(2), 130-136.

Reissman, C. (1993). *Narrative analysis.* Newbury Park, CA: Sage.

Ribbens McCarthy, J. (2006). *Young people's experiences of loss and bereavement: Towards an interdisciplinary approach.* Maidenhead, Berkshire: McGraw-Hill Education.

Robinson, G. (2000). *Essential Judaism: A complete guide to beliefs, customs, and rituals.* New York, NY: Pocket Books.

Rogers, J., Alex, M., MacDonald, C., Gallant, D., & Austin, W. (2009). Working with children in end-of-life decision making. *Nursing Ethics, 16*(6), 744-758.

Rosdahl, C., & Kowalski, M. (2008). *Textbook of basic nursing.* USA: Lippincott Williams & Wilkins.

Roshi, J. (2006). A Buddhist's perspective on grieving. *Explore, 2*(3), 260-261.

Ross, H. (2001). Islamic tradition at the end of life. *Medsurg Nursing, 10*(2), 83-87.

Ross, T. (2012). *A survival guide for health research methods.* New York, NY: Open University Press.

Rothaupt, J. & Becker, K. (2007). A literature review of western bereavement theory: From decathecting to continuing bonds. *The Family Journal: Counseling and Therapy for Couples and Families, 15*(1), 6-15.

Rowling, L., & Holland, J. (2000). Grief and school communities: The impact of social context, a comparison between Australia and England. *Death Studies, 24*(1), 35-50.

Runeson, B., & Asberg, M. (2003). Family history of suicide among suicide victims. *The American Journal of Psychiatry, 160*(8), 1525-1526.

Runeson, I., Enskar, K., Elander, G., & Hermeren, G. (2001). Professionals' perceptions of children's participation in decision making in healthcare. *Journal of Clinical Nursing, 10*(1), 70-78.

Rutter, M. (1966). *Children of sick parents.* London: Oxford University Press.

Saldinger, A., Cain, A., Kalter, N., & Lohnes, K. (1999). Anticipating parental death in families with young children. *American Journal of Orthopsychiatry, 69*(1), 39-48.

Sandelowski, M. (1995). Focus on qualitative methods: Sample size in qualitative research. *Research in Nursing and Health, 18,* 179-183.

Schonfeld, D., & Quackenbush, M. (2009). *After a loved one dies: How children grieve and how parents and other adults can support them.* New York, NY: New York Life Foundation.

Schuurman, D. (2003). *Never the same: Coming to terms with the death of a parent*. New York: St. Martin's Press.
Scott, C. (2004). *Children's grief theory: A critical literature review*. Unpublished master's thesis, Pacific University, Forest Grove, Oregon.
Shapiro, E. R. (1996). Family bereavement and cultural diversity: A social developmental perspective. *Family Process, 35*(3), 313-332.
Sharma, D. (1990). Hindu attitude toward suffering, dying and death. *Palliative Medicine, 4*(3), 235-238.
Sheikh, A. (1998). Death and dying - A Muslim perspective. *Journal of the Royal Society of Medicine, 91*, 138-140.
Shepherd, D., & Barraclough, B. (1976). The aftermath of parental suicide for children. *British Journal of Psychiatry, 129*, 267-276.
Silverman, P. (2000). *Never too young to know: Death in children's lives*. New York: Oxford University Press.
Silverman, P., Baker, J., Cait, C., & Boerner, K. (2003). The effects of negative legacies on the adjustment of parentally bereaved children and adolescents. *OMEGA, 46*(4), 335-352.
Silverman, P. R., & Worden, J. W. (1992). Children's reactions in the early months after the death of a parent. *American Journal of Orthopsychiatry, 62*(1), 93-104.
Slaughter, V. (2005). Young children's understanding of death. *Australian Psychologist, 40*(3), 179-186.
Smith, S. (1999). *Guidelines for working with bereaved children*. (2nd ed.). England: Jessica Kingsley Publishers Ltd.
Solomon, R. M., & Rando, T. A. (2014). Utilisation of eye movement desensitisation and reprocessing in the treatment of grief and mourning. *Bereavement Care, 33*(3), 118- 126. doi: 10.1080/02682621.2014.98098
Speece, M., & Brent, S. (1984). Children's understanding of death: A review of three components of a death concept. *Child Development, 55*(5), 1671-1686.
Spiro, H., Curnen, M., & Wandel, L. (1996). *Facing death*. New Haven, CT: Yale University.
Steen, K. (1998). A comprehensive approach to bereavement. *The Nurse Practitioner, 23*(2), 54-68.
Stokes, J. (2009). Resilience and bereaved children. *Bereavement Care, 28*(1), 9-17. doi: 10.1080/02682620902746078
Stoppelbein, L., & Greening, L. (2000). Posttraumatic stress symptoms in parentally bereaved children and adolescents. *Journal of the American Academy of Child and Adolescent Psychiatry, 39*(9), 1112-1119.
Suad, J. (2006). *Encyclopedia of women and Islamic cultures*. Netherlands: Koninklijke Brill.
Taylor, S. G., & Bogdan, R. (1984). *Introduction to qualitative research methods: The search for meanings* (2nd ed.). New York: Wiley.
Thakrar, D., & Aery, A. (2008). *Death and bereavement*. New York, NY: Radcliffe Medical Press.
Tindall, B. (1999). *Supporting sick children and their families*. London, EN: Harcourt Publishers Limited.
Tremblay, G., & Israel, A. (1998). Children's adjustment to parental death. *American Psychological Association, 5*(4), 424-438.
United Nations General Assembly. (2002). *A world fit for children: Resolution adopted by the general assembly*. New York: United Nations General Assembly.
Wada, K., & Parl, J. (2009). Integrating psychology into grief counselling. *Death Studies, 33*(7), 657-683.
Walsh, K., King, M., Jones, L., Tookman, A., & Blizard, R. (2005). Spiritual beliefs may affect outcome of bereavement: Prospective study. *British Medical Journal, 324*(7353), 1551-1554.
Washington, S. (2010). *Entering the griever's tunnel*. USA: Smashwords.
Webb, N. (2010). *Helping bereaved children: A handbook for practitioners*. New York, NY: The Guilford Press.
Werner-Lin, A., & Biank, N. (2013). Holding parents so they can hold their children: Grief work with surviving spouses to support parentally bereaved children. *Omega: Journal of Death and Dying, 66*(1), 1-16. doi: 10.2190/OM.66.1.a

References

White, J. M., Martin, T. F., & Bartolic, S.K. (2013). *Families Across the Life Course.* Toronto, CA: Pearson.

Willis, C. A. (2002). The grieving process in children: Strategies for understanding, educating, and reconciling children's perception of death. *Early Childhood Education Journal, 29*(4), 221-227.

Wolchik, S., Ma, Y., Tein, J., Sandler, I., & Ayers, T. (2008). Parentally bereaved children's grief: Self-system beliefs as mediators of the relations between grief and stressors and caregiver-child relationship quality. *Death Studies, 32*(7), 597-620.

Wolfelt, A. (1983). *Helping children cope with grief.* Muncie, IN: Accelerated Development.

Wolfenstein, M. (1966). How is mourning possible? *Psychoanalytic Study of the Child, 21,* 93-126.

Worchel, D., & Gearing, R. (2010). *Suicide assessment and treatment.* New York, NY: Springer Publishing Company, LLC.

Worden, J. (2009). Chapter 4: Grief counseling: Facilitating uncomplicated grief. In *Grief counseling and grief therapy* (pp. 83-126). New York: Springer Publishing Company.

Worden, J., & Silverman, P. (1993). Grief and depression in newly widowed parents with school-age children. *OMEGA, 27,* 251-260.

Yin, R., (1994). *Case study research: Design and methods* (2nd ed.). Beverly Hills, CA: Sage Publishing.

Zisook, S., & Shear, K. (2009). Grief and bereavement: What psychiatrists need to know. *World Psychiatry, 8*(2), 67–74.

Zonnebelt-Smeenge, S., & De Vries, R. (2006). *Traveling through grief: Learning to live again after the death of a loved one.* USA: Baker Books.

www.ingramcontent.com/pod-product-compliance
Lightning Source LLC
Chambersburg PA
CBHW062027290426
44108CB00025B/2804